THE CELESTIAL JOURNEY AND THE HARMONY OF THE SPHERES

in English Literature 1300 - 1700

by

CARRIE ESTHER HAMMIL

Published by
Texas Christian University Press
Fort Worth, Texas

Library of Congress Cataloging in Publication Data

Hammil, Carrie E
  The celestial journey and the harmony of the spheres.

  Bibliography: p. 00
  1. English literature—Early modern, 1500-1700—
History and criticism. 2. English literature—Middle English, 1100-1500—History and criticism. 3. Harmony of the spheres in literature. 4 Dreams in literature. 5. Voyages, Imaginary—History and criticism.
I. Title.
PR409.H37H35 1980   820'.9'353   79-28416
ISBN 0-912646-53-5 pbk.

Produced and Distributed by
Monograph Publishing
Carrollton Press, Inc.
1911 Fort Myer Drive
Arlington, VA 22209

Dedicated to
the Memory of my Beloved Parents,
Fred W. and Charlotta M. Hammil,
who, during the early writing of
this book, joined the heavenly
choir.

CONTENTS

INTRODUCTION

Esther Hammil's plan for this book was bold. She intended to extend her study into the nineteenth century. She meant to deal with the aesthetic concomitants of the celestial journey and its accompanying harmony of the spheres: with the harmony of the spectrum into white light, with the Aeolian wind harp as perfect harmony untouched by human hands. She hoped to deal with the appearance of the entire concept in literatures other than English. She wanted to write on Dante and his Italian colleagues and followers, to go into French literature where the concept is especially abounding in the sixteenth century, to delve into the literatures and the sciences of Islam.

The title that the author proposed for the projected, extended work was The Way on High: The Celestial Journey and the Harmony of the Spheres as a Motif in Literature.

Ill health cut short Dr. Hammil's teaching career. Bedfast and blind, she could not pursue her research and writing. Though she did much study in the pre-Romantics and Romantics of English literature, it seemed best to conclude this particular study with the year 1700.

In recent years Dr. Hammil has received the help of Dr. John Gregory, who began working with her while he was a graduate student at Texas Christian University, where she was granted the doctor's degree. A musicologist member of the TCU faculty, David Graham, gave attention to the editorial preparation of the text and monitored the passages that deal with the science and history of music.

Dr. Hammil has a special feeling of gratitude for Dr. Alan M. F. Gunn, who has given her encouragement and help in her studies and writing. Dr. Gunn is author of the Epilogue, which brings together some of

i

the ideas that she wanted to develop. Dr. Gunn has worked closely with the TCU Press in bringing the book to completion.

Dr. Hammil writes: "I wish to extend my thanks to the library staff of Texas Christian University for the many ways they have assisted me in obtaining the material needed, for some of it was quite elusive.

"My thanks go also to the following who have granted special permission to use illustrations or quotations in the book: The New York Times News Service for permission to quote from Archibald Macleish's article, "Mankind's Image May be Remade"; John Van Doren, Executive Editor, The Great Ideas Today, for permission to adapt the Johannes Kepler charts; the University of North Carolina Press for permission to use the illustration from Vincenzo Cartari's Le Imagini dei Dei Degli Antichi; and the University of Chicago Press for permission to use the illustration, "The Structure of the Desana Cosmos."

"I wish also to express my loving appreciation for the devotion and faith shown by my parents throughout my life and through these years of study. Had they not inspired me early with the vision of Heaven and the deep faith in God through which I have found the strength He gives to me, this book would not have been possible. My only regret is that they did not live to see it completed."

On behalf of all those who have known Dr. Hammil and worked with her I express gratitude and admiration. This expression will extend also, perhaps, to future scholars who will build on the foundation that she lays here.

James Newcomer, Director
Texas Christian University Press

Vincenzio Cartari's Interpretation of
Necessity, the Spindle, and Her Daughters

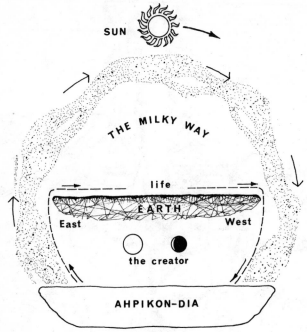

SUN

THE MILKY WAY

life

EARTH

East West

the creator

AHPIKON-DIA

The Structure of the Desana Cosmos

An Amazonian Indian Concept of the Universe
According to Gerardo Reichel-Dolmatoff

CHAPTER I

THE HARMONY OF THE SPHERES IN ANTIQUITY

From the time that man first looked toward the skies at night, his imagination has carried him along a glowing pathway that stretches across that space, often to the accompaniment of the much-fabled "Harmony of the Spheres." From that pathway he has viewed his earth and the universe, thereby striving to attain the perspective he needs for a truer view of his relationship with God and his fellow men. In this search for the knowledge that leads to perfect harmony, man has looked upon the universe from the spot he conceives to be its center--whether it be Babylon, Jerusalem, a particular temple, or (as in certain traditions of early Christianity) Golgotha. Ovid tells us that "though all other animals are prone, and fix their gaze upon the earth, [God] gave to man an uplifted face and bade him stand erect and turn his eyes to heaven."[1] Ovid, and those of whom he tells us, saw Jove looking down from "a high way, easily seen when the sky is clear. 'Tis called the Milky Way, famed for its shining whiteness."[2] This "via sublimis," Ovid tells us, is the way to the dwelling of Jove. "On either side the palaces of the gods of higher rank are thronged with guests through folding-doors flung wide. The lesser gods dwell apart from these. Fronting on this way, the illustrious and strong heavenly gods have placed their homes. This is the place which, if I may make bold to say it, I would not fear to call the Palatia of high heaven."[3]

Dominating a long train of legends and traditions is a picture of the Milky Way as the path to Heaven which, if traveled by a thoughtful man, may enable him to attain perspective in his views of the world and of himself

1

Near the end of The Republic, Plato tells the story of Er, son of Armenius. Felled in battle, he lay untended for ten days before his body was placed upon a funeral pyre. Two days later, while lying in state upon that pyre, Er returned to life and told what he had seen in the next world, of tenfold punishments for sins, of glad reunions in a meadow, of eternal punishment of tyrants. Then, said Er, those spirits who were permitted to gather in the meadow were brought on a journey. They "came to a place where they could see from above a line of light, straight as a column, extending right through the whole heaven and through the earth, in colour resembling the rainbow, only brighter and purer."[4] Another day they traveled; and now, as they drew closer to the column of light, they saw in the midst of it "the ends of the chain of heaven let down from above: for this light is the belt of heaven, and holds together the circumference of the universe, like the under-girders of a trireme."[5] At this point we begin to see a merging of Images: the Milky Way as a supporting band of the universe and the cosmic pillar or mountain (golden chain, Jacob's ladder, etc.) of communication, as well as the Great Chain of Being upon which all members of Creation have their place and rank.

Plato then has Er describe the organization of the universe. The "spindle of Necessity, on which all the revolutions turn," extends from the ends of this chain, with large, hollowed-out "whorls" each fitted inside the next in graduated sizes, "making eight in all, like vessels which fit into one another; the whorls show their circular edges on the upper side, and on their lower side all together form one continuous whorl."[6] All of this is pierced by the spindle, "which is driven home through the centre of the eighth."[7] The outermost of the whorls, that of the fixed stars, is spangled. "The spindle turns on the knees of Necessity; and on the upper surface of each circle stands a siren, who goes round with them, chanting a single tone or note."[8] Together, the eight form one concordance or harmony. Sitting around them, "at equal intervals," are three other figures—the Fates, daughters of Necessity, clothed in white. These three sing with the sirens to accompany them; Lachesis sings of the past, Clotho of the present, and Atropos of the future. They also assist their mother, Necessity, in turning the spindle. Clotho gives a touch of her hand now and again to the outer circle or to the spindle itself. Atropos uses her left hand to guide the inner spheres, while Lachesis takes turns with either hand to guide inner or outer turnings. The inner whorls turn in the direction opposite to the outer one.

A number of Renaissance dictionaries contain discussions and illustrations of Plato's conception of Necessity, her spindle, and her daughters. The following illustration is from Le Imagini dei Dei degli Antichi by Vincenzio Cartari, the Latin version of which was Antoine du Verdier's Imagines Deorum.[9] In essence, Le Imagini follows Plato's description, although it omits his passage concerning the parts played by the three sisters in helping to turn the spheres. In fact, the spheres themselves are not shown, nor does he mention the sirens riding the spheres and producing the harmony. Necessity, on an elevated throne, holds the spindle; and her daughters, wearing crowns in Cartari's illustration, assist in its turning in accord with Plato's description.[10]

Er, in his visit to the afterworld, accompanied the other souls downwards to the place where Lachesis directed them to choose their next lives. Er, however, was set aside; and when the others drank of the River of Forgetfulness to remove their former lives from their memory, Er again was restrained so that as the others "were driven upwards in all manner of ways to their birth, like stars shooting,"[11] he awoke on the funeral pyre with full memory of all that he had seen.

Plato says that we should "hold fast ever to the heavenly way and follow after justice and virtue always, considering that the soul is immortal and able to endure every sort of good and every sort of evil. . . . And it shall be well with us both in this life and in the pilgrimage of a thousand years which we have been describing."[12] Here Plato's philosophical intent

science, presents an astronomical theory that resembles that of the
Pythagoreans in some ways and differs from it in others. Pythagoras (582
B.C.--after 507) was first of all a mathematician. Born in Syria, later
spending more than twenty years in Egypt and another dozen years in Babylon,
he then settled in Samos, bringing to the Greeks the doctrine of the Harmony
of the Spheres. The immense popularity of this doctrine was related to the
seemingly divine orderliness of number which had been revealed in musical
tones. Pythagoras' great interest in music arose from his fascination with
numbers and was not directed toward music as a practical art. He had
learned--in Egypt or Babylon, probably--that if a vibrating string of any
length were divided into halves, thirds, fourths, etc., the resulting tones
(overtones, or harmonics) always bore a fixed intervallic relationship to the
fundamental tone produced by the whole string. Thus a division into halves
produced the octave, division into thirds produced the twelfth (octave plus
a fifth), division into fourths produced the double octave (twelfth plus a
fourth), and so on. If all the tones, beginning with the fundamental pitch,
are numbered, then the interval (distance in pitch) between any two tones
could be expressed as the mathematical ratio of their respective string
lengths. And so octaves have a ratio of 1:2, fifths are 2:3, fourths are
3:4, major (large) thirds are 4:5, minor (small) thirds are 5:6, and major
seconds are 8:9.

Pythagoras theorized that each planet in addition to the sphere of
the Fixed Stars produced its own tone, the result of the motion of the spheres.
He also believed that the relative rates of motion and the resulting tones
had the same ratios as those found in the vibrating string, thus producing
the Harmony of the Spheres. But his attempts to prove this theory were not
successful. We do not hear these cosmic tones, he maintained, because we
have heard them so continually from birth that our ears no longer perceive
them. Plato appears to have felt it at least allegorically necessary to give
these sounds an organic rather than a mechanical origin in the embodiment of
singing sirens riding on the surface of the "whorls" or spheres as they turn:

Pythagoras had shown, however, that "the invisible fluid of sound [contained] hidden mathematics. The kinships that man's ear recognized were nothing but relationships among numbers, the harmony of vibrations. The human ear proved to be in tune with nature, linked with nature by a mathematical mystery."[13]

One of the most complete records we have of early Greek thought with respect to the conception of the universe is contained in Aristotle's De Caelo.[14] Here, Plato's pupil examines the theories of his forerunners, testing and proving, substantiating and refuting their ideas, always with a view to practical objectivity. A chief concern of Aristotle is to study the need for something or someone to impart motion to the spheres and their planets or to support them to keep them from falling from their place, a concern we find reflected many centuries later in the writings of Johannes Kepler. Aristotle comes to the conclusion that because the outermost heaven is eternal and perfect, it itself cannot involve effort. Therefore, he maintains, the myth that Atlas bears the earth upon his shoulders, the theory that whirling overcomes the effect of weight, and the idea that a soul causes motion are all impossible.

In Chapter 9, Book 2, of De Caelo Aristotle refutes Pythagoras' concept of the Harmony of the Spheres as a physical reality. The Pythagorean theory, he says, is based upon a belief that motion is always accompanied by sound and that this sound must vary in intensity and frequency directly with respect to the size of the moving body. Pythagoras' conception requires further, says Aristotle, that the intervals between the planets and the Sphere of the Fixed Stars have the same mathematical proportion as the intervals of the musical consonances. The sound produced within such a system would have a concordant quality. Aristotle's reply that the theory "shows great feeling for fitness and beauty" gives us our most important clue to its attractiveness to poets for many centuries afterward.[15] However, he contends, any sound made by an object as large as that of a heavenly body would be a deafening roar to which even long exposure from birth would not make one oblivious, as the Pythagoreans had proposed. Such a sound would in fact be damaging. Moreover, things carried within a vessel (like the planets within their spheres) do not make a sound as the ship carries them along; and if a ship is moving downstream, it does so soundlessly. What does make sound, he explains, "is that which is moving in a stationary medium. If the medium is in motion continuous with that of the object, and produces no impact, there cannot be noise."[16]

Although the original idea of the Harmony of the Spheres has been ascribed to Pythagoras, the fact that all such references have come to us through other writers and over a span of many centuries makes its exact origin by no means certain. Pliny the Elder (23 - 79 A.D.), in the Natural History, sets forth the harmonic intervals between the heavenly bodies thus:

Earth to Moon = one tone

Moon to Mercury = a semitone

Mercury to Venus = a semitone

Venus to Sun = a minor third

Sun to Mars = one tone

Mars to Jupiter = a semitone

Jupiter to Saturn = a semitone

Saturn to the Zodiac or Fixed Stars = a tone and half
(minor third).[17]

Just as Aristotle gives us an historical resume of the theories of the system of the universe in De Caelo, so in Meteorologica he presents a review and discussion of more specific phenomena, including shooting stars, comets, the Aurora Borealis, and the Milky Way. Here, he refutes many of the views of his day and earlier, including one that postulated that the Milky Way was but a reflection of our vision to the sun. It can be seen reflected in waters or mirrors, contends Aristotle, and therefore must be actual and not merely itself an image. He believes that the Milky Way comprises a great circle dividing the heavens along the solstitial colure.[18] There, hot and dry exhalations under the influence of the fixed stars are continually being ignited and consumed in much the same manner as that by which he conceives

of comets being formed; so it seems likely that the Milky Way is formed of
the same material that is to be formed in the tails of comets. The conception
of the Milky Way as a circle coinciding with the zones of the solstices is
one to be found in a number of pre-Christian and primitive cultures. As
such, it is highly coincident with the idea of a cosmic pillar that provides
a concourse to the gods, of which the Milky Way is the visible image. This
pillar or concourse is said to support and separate the three levels of the
universe—underworld, earth, and the heavens. By means of this way on high,
passage is possible from one of these levels to another. This conception has
its counterparts in a number of center-of-the-universe images, including such
cosmic mountains as Dante's Mount of Purgatory and its opposing inverted
construction of Hell; and it is frequently combined with Jacob's ladder as
means of communication with Heaven. Temples in many traditions and religions
have followed this train of thought, serving as links between the world of
men and the realm of God. The ceremonial Cosmic Tree is another example of
the way of ascent, represented in some instances by a supporting pole in a
tent used for religious ceremonies and by means of which the celebrants
aspire to ascend to communication with Heaven.[19] These ideas concerning the
Milky Way-Cosmic Pillar image appear to be archetypal. In a study of the
Desana Indians, a subgroup of the Tukano tribe in the upper Amazon basin of
Columbia, Gerardo Reichel-Dolmatoff has discovered a complex and well defined
pattern of belief, shown in the accompanying diagram. It is very close in
its fundamental ideas to some of the principles laid down by Plato, especially
those concerning the creative role of the Demlurge. The creator of the
universe is called page abe, the Sun Father, and is non-created, a "state"
of yellow light, "not the same sun which now illuminates our earth but a
creative principle" of which our sun is "the eternal representative."[20]
The Creation of the Sun Father contains three cosmic zones—the upper or
celestial, the intermediate or terrestrial, and the lower zone of Paradise.
"The most important structural component of the upper zone "is the Milky Way.
The Milky Way is conceived of as a large skein of fibers of the cumare

palm (Astrocaryum) that floats in a turbulent current arching over the earth. This current is called mirúnye bagá / 'wind skein,' and comes from the lower zone, flowing from east to west."[21] For the Desanas and the Tukanos, of whom they are part the Milky Way is the zone of communication between earthly and supernatural beings by means of hallucinations or visions; and it is the habitat of a divine power personified as the Vihó-mahsé, who, "in a state of perpetual trance, travels along this celestial way observing the earth and its inhabitants."[22]

Mircea Eliade explains that "such a cosmic pillar can be only at the very center of the universe, for the whole of the habitable world extends around it." He calls it a "system of the world" in which "(a) a sacred place constitutes a break in the homogeneity of space; (b) this break is symbolized by an opening by which passage from one cosmic region to another is made possible . . . (c) communication with heaven is expressed by one or another of certain images, all of which refer to the axis mundi . . . (d) around this cosmic axis lies the world (= our world), hence . . . it is the Center of the World."[23]

These intervals all are based upon the early conceptions of the distances from Earth to the moon and thence to the spheres of the other planets and upon the mathematical ratios of those distances. Pliny and Censorinus both state that Pythagoras believed the moon's distance from earth to be 126,000 stadia. (A stade is equal to 516.73 feet.)[24] Ptolemy, in the second century A.D., compared the angles between planets with musical intervals. The angle of 180°, being opposition or a straight line, equaled the octave; 120°, a fifth; 90°, a quadrature, was equal to the interval of a fourth; and 60° equaled a second. Dreyer points out that "the whole doctrine is quite analogous to that of astrology, but is vastly more exalted in its conception than the latter, and it deserves honourable mention in the history of human progress."[25]

Important to writers of the Mediaeval and Renaissance periods were a group of encyclopedists of the fourth, fifth, and sixth centuries who

epitomized--and in some cases were the sole preservers of--certain classical
writings, especially those that they found philosophically attractive. The
list includes Boethius, Martianus Capella, Cassiodorus, Isidore of Seville,
and--of great importance to us at this point--Macrobius. It is to Macrobius--
Macrobius Ambrosius Theodosius--that we are indebted for the preservation of
Cicero's Somnium Scipionis, the sixth book of De Re Publica, to which
Macrobius appended his own commentary. The Somnium and some scattered
fragments of others of the six books of De Re Publica were all that were
known of the work until other sections and some of these as well were found
in the Vatican Library in 1820, included in a manuscript of Augustine's
commentary on the Psalms. For writers in the centuries prior to the nineteenth, then, Macrobius' Commentary was the sole source for Cicero's Somnium
Scipionis. It is no wonder that some (including Chaucer for a time) thought
him to be its author.

De Re Publica was written by Cicero beginning probably in May of
54 B.C., at about the time, according to Clinton Walker Keyes, when the
transfer of his authority to the First Triumvirate "gave him the leisure to
follow in the footsteps of his beloved Plato by composing a second Republic."[26]
A discourse concerning the operations of government and the affairs of the
commonwealth, De Re Publica consists of dialogues supposedly taking place
during the Latin holidays of 129 B.C. in the garden of Scipio--Pubilus
Cornelius Scipio Africanus the Younger.[27] A number of consuls and philosophers
discuss forms of government, justice, and social classes, and on two of the
days (each book is supposed to represent a day's conversation) they deal
with matters of the universe. With a keen sense for form and structure in
his writing, Cicero opens and closes De Re Publica with discussions of
celestial matters. In Book I, with a conversation about astronomy in general
and Archimedes' celestial globe, he sets forth the comparative importance of
heavenly and earthly matters for study. In Book VI, with the dream of Scipio,
he extends all that the company has talked about to a point beyond earth and
into the universe.

In structure and in organization, a definite imitation of Plato's Republic may be seen. Most important for us, however, is the use of the model supplied by Plato's myth of Er, with certain differences in application. While both Plato and Cicero utilize the dream device as a means of concluding a treatise on the ideal republic, Cicero differs from Plato in making Scipio recount a dream rather than come back to life and recount his experiences during "death" as Er had done. F. E. Rockwood says, "Plato resorted to the fabulous and miraculously restored the dead to life. Cicero adopts a more natural plan and is thereby more effective. . . . Cicero's good taste in preferring the dream to any other less human and less natural method of revelation . . . [has] been deservedly commended by the critics."[28]

Young Scipio, then a military tribune in the Fourth Legion in Africa (149 B.C.), has been spending an evening reminiscing with King Masinissa, an old friend of his adoptive grandfather, Publius Cornelius Scipio Africanus the Elder. When he retires for the night, he dreams of his grandfather, who tells him of his future achievements, campaigns, and dangers. When Scipio asks about life after death, his father, Aemilius Paulus, joins them, explaining to Scipio that "vestra vero, quae dicitur, vita mors est." The soul is truly alive, Macrobius explains in the Commentary, when it is in the realms above the moon; and life in a mortal body is the soul's death, so that, as Scipio's father has told him, that which we call the true life is really a living death. This concept is prevalent through the poetry of many centuries. When Scipio, however, wishes to die and go to them at once instead of waiting, he is told that all the sky that he can see is God's temple. He may not enter it until God decrees. Man is given life in order that he might people "that sphere called Earth, which you see in the centre of this temple; and he has been given a soul out of those eternal fires which you call stars and planets, which, being round and globular bodies animated by divine intelligences, circle about in their fixed orbits with marvellous speed."[29] He must not abandon life of his own will lest he be guilty of shirking "the duty imposed upon man by God."[30]

Scipio then is shown a "circle of light which blazed most brightly among the other fires" called "the Milky Circle" (<u>orbem lacteum</u>).[31] "When I gazed in every direction from that point," Scipio says, "all else appeared wonderfully beautiful. There were stars which we never see from the earth, and they were all larger than we have ever imagined. The smallest of them was that farthest from heaven and nearest the earth which shone with a borrowed light. The starry spheres were much larger than the earth; indeed the earth itself seemed to me so small that I was scornful of our empire, which covers only a single point, as it were, upon its surface."[32] This last thought is central to the whole idea of dream visions concerning the Milky Way—that once man mounts upon that way on high and sees the universe in its true proportions, the things of this life seem small and insignificant to him and so transitory as to be but momentary in comparison with the eternity of Heaven.

A little later, Africanus elucidates still further this matter of man's time and God's as he tells Scipio, "For people commonly measure the year by the circuit of the sun, that is, of a single star alone; but when all the stars return to the place from which they at first set forth, and, at long intervals, restore the original configuration of the whole heaven, then that can truly be called a revolving [or great] year."[33] This principle is also found in Plato's <u>Timaeus</u> 39, and Cicero discusses it again in <u>De Natura Deorum</u>, <u>Academica</u> II, 51.

The astronomical system delineated by Cicero differs somewhat from the usual classical arrangement. For him, the outermost sphere, which he calls <u>caelestis</u> (the Celestial) is itself the supreme God and contains all the rest. He describes the sun as "almost midway the distance" between Heaven and Earth and as "the lord, chief, and ruler of the other lights, the mind and guiding principle of the universe, of such magnitude that he reveals and fills all things with his light."[34] Venus and Mercury he places below the sun "in their orbits" but does not say which is in which of those two spheres. It is of interest here also that Cicero says that the sun is almost midway between Heaven and Earth, making its position analogous to that of the _mese_, the middle note of the scale of tones comprising the so-called Greater Perfect System of Greek music.

It is a frequent topic of discussion that Cicero in this instance numbers the spheres from the outside toward Earth, contrary to general practice. He refers to Earth, for example, as "_media et nona_."[35] However, it must be remembered that it is his character-guide, Africanus, who is speaking and that Africanus and Scipio are standing in the Milky Way so that Earth is the farthest from them, not the nearest. Africanus would naturally count outward from the point where he himself is standing. This becomes especially important when we reach a discussion of some of Chaucer's works.

Macrobius, in his _Commentary on the Dream of Scipio_, has a great deal more to say about the Milky Way, much of it very important to later poets and prose writers, who are evidence of his immense popularity in later ages. In Chapter XII, for example, he is concerned with "the order of the steps by which the soul descends from the sky to the infernal regions of this life." The Milky Way "girdles the zodiac" and crosses it at the two tropical signs, Capricorn and Cancer, which Homer calls the "portals of the sun."[36] The solstices, explains Macrobius, lie across the path of the sun so that the sun must go back and forth across its path and not beyond those limits. Souls pass through these portals when going from the sky to earth and returning, descending through Cancer (thus the portal of men) and returning to the heavenly abode through Capricorn (the portal of the gods). And he tells us that "Pythagoras also thinks that the infernal regions of Dis begin with the Milky Way." An interesting comment, which Macrobius also credits to Pythagoras, is that "the reason why milk is the first nourishment offered to the newborn infant is that the first movement of souls slipping into earthly bodies is from the Milky Way."[37] All of this is remarkably close to the traditions of the Desana Cosmos discussed earlier, reminding us once more of the universality of these concepts.

As he stood in the Milky Way and watched and listened in astonishment, Scipio tells his listeners, he became aware of a strange sound. "What is this loud and agreeable sound that fills my ears?" he asks.

"'That is produced,' Africanus replies, 'by the onward rush and motion of the spheres themselves; the intervals between them, though unequal, being exactly arranged in a fixed proportion, by an agreeable blending of high and low tones, various harmonies are produced.'"[38] Although Cicero modeled his De Re Publica as a whole after Plato's Republic, there are no sirens riding the spheres and humming the tones. As in the theories of the Pythagoreans, the music comes from the spheres themselves and from the mathematical ratios existing among them. The uppermost sphere, that of the Fixed Stars, moves most rapidly, Africanus explains, and therefore emits a high, shrill tone, whereas the Moon, as the slowest, sounds the lowest. "But the other eight spheres, two of which move with the same velocity, produce seven different sounds,--a number which is the key of almost everything."[39] Unlike Pliny, Cicero gives no hint as to the exact intervals between the tones thus produced. Macrobius, however, sets forth a detailed explanation of the Pythagorean concept of the importance of proportion:

[4] Since we have explained the order of the spheres and have pointed out how the seven underlying spheres rotate in the opposite direction to the celestial sphere's motion, it is fitting for us next to investigate the sounds produced by the onrush of such vast bodies. [5] From the very rotation of the spheres sound must come forth because air, when lashed, at the very instant of the blow sends forth from itself the force of the contact, as is natural; thus a violent crashing of two bodies ends in a noise. But a sound produced by any lashing of air comes to the ears as something either sweet and melodious or dissonant and harsh. [6] An agreeable concord results when the percussion is in keeping with certain numerical relations, but a grating discord results from a random blow, lacking proportionate intervals. [7] Now it is well known that in the heavens nothing happens by chance or at random, and that all things above proceed in orderly fashion according to divine law. Therefore it is unquestionably right to assume that harmonious sounds come forth from the rotation of the heavenly spheres, for sound has to come from motion, and Reason, which is present in the divine, is responsible for sounds being

melodious.[40]

He gives the "consonant chords" as the fourth, fifth, octave-and-a-fifth, and double octave. "This number of consonant chords has to do only with the music that the human breath can produce or the human ear can catch; beyond this there is still the range of celestial harmony, which reaches even four times the octave and fifth."[41]

Now, these are the same as those numerical ratios that Plato, in the Timaeus, said were used by God in the construction of the World Soul: a portion of the whole mixture of the monad, the source of even (male) and uneven (female) numbers, plus a second portion double the first, then one one-and-a-half times the second and three times the first, a fourth portion double the second, a fifth three times the third, a sixth eight times the first, and a seventh twenty-seven times the first.[42] "This monad," Macrobius tells us, "the beginning and ending of all things, yet itself not knowing a beginning or ending, refers to the Supreme God," and is also the Mind, "sprung from the Supreme God," unnumbered but producing and containing "innumerable patterns of created things."[43] Using the numeral 2 to represent the monad, and reducing the operations to simple multiplications of this unit, we can present this pattern diagrammatically as follows:

$$1$$

1X2 (2nd)	1X3 (3rd)
1X4 (4th)	1X9 (5th)
1X8 (6th)	1X27 (7th)

It will be seen that the second, fourth, and sixth steps are in a doubling progression; the third, fifth, and seventh tripling.

We are told, further, that the intervals between these steps were filled in with others in the ratios of 3:2, 4:3, and 9:8, which Plato, in the Timaeus, says are "not wholly dissoluble save by Him who had bound them together."[45] It will be recalled that 3:2 is the ratio of the interval of a fourth, 4:3 is the ratio of the fifth, and the two form the Diapason or

octave. It should also be remembered, of course, that Plato is interested in
these proportions and intervals for mathematical and philosophical speculation,
not for the practical study of music as an art. At the same time, however,
we know that he had the Pythagorean concept in mind and that he no doubt
intended at least metaphorically to equate the mathematical and philosophical
ideas. All of this casts considerable light on the relationship among the
Harmony of the Spheres, the World Soul, and the Octave System of the seven-
stringed lyre which stands as their earthly image.[46] Macrobius sums it all
up in this way:

> Hence we clearly see that these words of Cicero's [i.e.,
> Scipio's query about 'this great and pleasing sound' and
> Africanus' reply] would never have been comprehensible if we
> had not included a discussion of the sesquialters [interval
> of a fifth, ratio 3:2], sesquitertians [interval of a fourth,
> 4:3], and superoctaves inserted in the intervals, and of the
> numbers with which Plato constructed the World-Soul, together
> with the reason why the Soul was interwoven with numbers
> producing harmony. In so doing we have not only explained
> the revolutions in the heavens, for which the Soul alone is
> responsible; we have also shown that the sounds which arose
> from these had to be harmonious, for they were innate in the
> Soul which impelled the universe to motion.[47]

The ratios here given for the World Soul will furthermore be seen as being
concordant with those given earlier (p. 4) for musical overtones and the
Harmony of the Spheres. As Macrobius explains, of the three scales used by
the Greeks, i.e., the Enharmonic, the Diatonic, and the Chromatic, the first
was discarded as too difficult and the third "because it induces voluptuous-
ness." Hence, the Diatonic is the one chosen by Plato for celestial harmony.[48]

Johannes de Verwere (Tinctoris), a Flemish musical theorist who
lived from 1446 to 1511, wrote in regard to his studies of musical thought,
"I will not hide the fact that I have studied what the ancient philosophers,
such as Plato and Pythagoras, as well as their successors, Cicero, Macrobius,
Boethius, and Isidore, believe concerning the harmony of the spheres. Since,
however, I have found that they differ very much from each other in their
teachings, I have turned from them to Aristotle and the more modern philosophers.

. . . The ancient musicians, Plato, Pythagoras, . . . and many others, . . .
dealt exclusively with the consonances, and yet we do not know at all how
they arranged and classified them."[49]   Cicero does, however, call our attention to the principle that the intervals are "though unequal . . . exactly
arranged in a fixed proportion." It is this mathematical unity that was to
prove so intriguing to poets to come; for, as Cicero continues, "Learned men,
by imitating this harmony on stringed instruments and in song, have gained
for themselves a return to this region, as others have obtained the same
reward by devoting their brilliant intellects to divine pursuits during their
earthly lives."[50]   Nor was this imitation to be restricted to the narrow confines of music alone.   It was to play a major part in the thoughts and writings
of poets and prose writers for centuries to come. Cicero's implied exclusion
here of wind instruments should be noted, for the resultant limitation becomes
important in much of literature. The wind instruments in some instances
become examples of discord, the stringed viols the epitome of concord. This
will be seen with great clarity in the works of Shakespeare, to give just one
example at this point.

Discussions of the nature and conformation of the universe itself
and of the philosophical concerpt of harmony were never separable. The soul
of the world and the soul of man have found their meeting ground in this
pattern of ideas. As we are told by Plato in the _Timaeus_, "For God desired
that, so far as possible, all things should be good and nothing evil; where-
fore, when He took over all that was visible, seeing that it was not in a
state of rest but in a state of discordant and disorderly motion, He brought
it into order out of disorder, deeming that the former state is in all ways
better than the latter. . . . Thus, then, . . . we must declare that this
Cosmos has verily come into existence as a Living Creature endowed with soul
and reason owing to the providence of God."[51]

NOTES

[1]Ovid, Metamorphoses, I. 84-86, ed. Frank Justus Miller (Cambridge, Massachusetts: Harvard University Press [Loeb Library], 1916, pp. 8-9. All references to Ovid are from this edition unless otherwise noted.

[2]Ibid., pp. 14-15.

[3]Ibid.

[4]The Dialogues of Plato, trans., B. Jowett, 4th ed. (Oxford: Clarendon Press, 1953), II, p. 494. All references to Plato's Republic are from this edition.

[5]Ibid.

[6]Republic, p. 494. The reader is also referred to Plato's Cosmology by Cornford, pp. 74-75 in which it is suggested that Plato is here discussing a model of armillary sphere which may have been before him as he wrote. (Francis MacDonald Cornford, Plato's Cosmology: The Timaeus of Plato Translated with a Running Commentary [London: Routledge and Kegan Paul, 1937].)

[7]Ibid, p. 494.

[8]Ibid., p. 495.

[9]De Witt Talmade Starnes and Ernest William Talbert, Classical Myth and Legend in Renaissance Dictionaries (Chapel Hill: University of North Carolina Press, 1955), p. 26.

[10]Ibid., pp. 369-371.

[11]Plato, Republic, p. 499.

[12]Ibid.

[13]Rudolph Thiel, And There Was Light, trans. by Richard and Clara Winston (New York, Alfred A. Knopf, 1957), p. 52.

[14]Aristotle, On the Heavens, trans. and ed., W. K. C. Guthrie

(Cambridge, Massachusetts: Harvard Univ. Press [Loeb Library], 1945). This
edition is hereafter cited as the Loeb edition.

[15] _On the Heavens_, Loeb edition, II. ix. pp. 195-197.

[16] Ibid.

[17] Pliny, _Natural History_, I, trans. and ed., H. Rackham (Cambridge,
Massachusetts: Harvard Univ. Press [Loeb Library], 1949) p. 228. All
references to Pliny's _Natural History_ are from this edition.

[18] Aristotle, _Meteorologica_, trans. and ed., W. K. C. Guthrie
(Cambridge, Massachusetts: Harvard Univ. Press [Loeb Library], 1942, I. viii.,
pp. 63-67. This edition is hereafter cited as the Loeb edition.

[19] Mircea Eliade, _Myths, Dreams and Mysteries_, trans., Philip Mairet
New York: Harper and Brothers, 1960), p. 64. The reader is especially
referred to Chapter V of this book, "Symbolisms of Ascension and 'Waking
Dreams'," in which the author discusses several archetypal examples of ascent
--"The Magic Flight," especially as it relates to the divinity of kings and
to the ecstatic soul-flight of religious mystics in many traditions; "The
Seven Steps of the Buddha" through the seven planetary heavens; and the
"Durohana and the 'Waking Dream'" especially as it relates to psychology.

[20] Gerardo Reichel-Dolmatoff, _Amazonian Cosmos: The Sexual and
Religious Symbolism of the Tukano Indians_ (Chicago: University of Chicago
Press, 1971), p. 41.

[21] Ibid., p. 43.

[22] Ibid., p. 43.

[23] Mircea Eliade, _The Sacred and the Profane: the Nature of Religion_,
trans. Willard R. Trask (New York: Harcourt, Brace and Company, 1959), p. 37.

Eliade's book, _The Myth of the Eternal Return_, published also under
the title, _Cosmos and History_, offers additional comment on the archetypal
nature of cosmic pillar imagery. It is sufficient for the purposes of the

present study to demonstrate that the idea has had its expression in many traditions in many places and at many times.

[24] H. C. King, Exploration of the Universe (New York: New American Library [Signet], 1964), p. 67.

[25] J. L. E. Dreyer, A History of Astronomy from Thales to Kepler, 2nd ed. (New York: Dover Publications, 1953), p. 181.

[26] Cicero, Marcus Tullius, De Re Publica, De Legibus, trans. and ed., Clinton Walker Keyes (Cambridge, Massachusetts: Harvard Univ. Press [Loeb Library], 1928, 1961), p. 2. This edition is hereafter cited as the Loeb edition.

[27] Ibid., p. 3.

[28] Cicero, Marcus Tullius, Tusculan Disputations I and Scipio's Dream, ed., Frank Ernest Rockwood (Norman: University of Oklahoma Press, 1903, 1966), pp. vii-viii. This edition is hereafter cited as the Rockwood edition.

[29] Loeb edition, VI. xv., pp. 266-267.

[30] Ibid., p. 269.

[31] Loeb edition, VI. xvi., pp. 268-269.

[32] Ibid.

[33] Loeb edition, VI. xxii, pp. 276-277.

[34] Ibid. VI. xvii, pp. 270-271.

[35] Ibid., VI. xvii, p. 270.

[36] Macrobius, Commentary on the Dream of Scipio, trans. and ed., William Harris Stahl (New York: Columbia Univ. Press, 1952), p. 133. Hereafter references to this edition of Macrobius will be cited as the Stahl edition.

[37] Ibid., fn. p. 134: "Porphyry (De antro nympharum xxviii) cites

Homer (Odyssey xxiv. 12) as the author of the name. Cf. Macrobius Saturnalia
I. xvii, 63; Helpericus of Auxerre De computo II (Migne Pat. Lat.,
CXXXVII, 25).

[38]Loeb edition, VI. xviii, pp. 270-271.

[39].Ibid, VI. xviii, pp. 272-273.

[40]Macrobius, Stahl edition, pp. 185-186. Stahl, in his footnotes
to this passage, refers the reader to a number of helpful comparisons with
the works of other writers, including but not restricted to Plato and
Aristotle. Stahl also comments on the familiar story of Pythagoras'
discovery of musical relationships in the blacksmith shop and points out
the fallacies involved.

[41]Ibid., p. 189.

[42]Plato, Timaeus, 36, in Plato With an English Translation, Volume
Vii, Timaeus, Critias, Cleitophon, Menexenus, Epistles, trans. and ed., The
Rev. R. G. Bury (London: William Heinemann; New York: G. P. Putnam's Sons,
1929 [Loeb Library]), p. 67. This edition is hereafter cited as Timaeus,
Loeb edition.

[43]Stahl edition, p. 101.

[44]Timaeus, Loeb edition, p. 66.

[45]Ibid., p. 97.

[46]From the seventh century B.C. onwards, archeological evidence
shows varying numbers of strings (from four to eleven or twelve) in con-
current use. . . . Terpander—a shadowy figure assigned to variant seventh-
century dates and suspiciously coupled with the mythical Olympus—was inflated
into a Founder of kitharistic [the kithara was a form of lyre] music, and
was supposed to have increased the strings of the phormix [another form of
lyre] from four to the symbolic number of seven, also imputed to Orpheus."
Isobel Henderson, "Ancient Greek Music," in The New Oxford History of Music,

Vol. I: <u>Ancient and Oriental Music</u>, ed. by Egon Wellesz (London: Oxford University Press, 1957) p. 381.

[47]Stahl edition, p. 193.

[48]Ibid., p. 199.

[49]Howard D. McKinney and W. R. Anderson, <u>Music in History</u> (New York: American Book Company, 1940), f.n., p. 210.

[50]<u>De Re Publica</u>, <u>De Legibus</u>, Loeb edition, VI. xviii, p. 273.

[51]<u>Timaeus</u>, Loeb edition, p. 55.

CHAPTER II

THE WAY TO MANY MANSIONS

"And I shall give wings to your mind which can carry
you aloft, so that, without further anxiety, you may return
safely to your own country under my direction, along my path,
and by my means. . . .

"My wings are swift, able to soar beyond the heavens.
The quick mind which wears them scorns the hateful earth and
climbs above the globe of the immense sky, leaving the clouds
below. . . . When it has seen enough, it flies beyond the
farthest sphere to mount the top of the swift heaven and share
the holy light.

"There the Lord of kings holds His scepter, governing
the reins of the world. With sure control He drives the swift
chariot, the shining judge of all things."

(Boethius, The Consolation of
Philosophy, IV; Prose 1, Poem 1.)[1]

There is a direct connection between man's ideas of the composition

of the physical universe and his relationship with God. As man turned

gradually away from the multiple deities who centered largely around nature

personification and toward the monotheistic view, his concepts of this

relationship between God and man also changed. Important in his thinking,

of course, were his ideas of the vast expanse of sky to which he directed

both his physical and his spiritual gaze.

A few of the thinkers of the early Christian centuries are so

prominent in their influence that some discussion of their thought is

necessary in order to understand that of their followers. One of the

earliest of these is Origen (or Origenes), who lived between approximately

23

185 and 254. He was one of the more controversial writers, and his works were both defended and refuted during his lifetime and long after. He produced an enormous number of treatises and commentaries on the Scriptures. For our purposes here, the most pertinent of the treatises is his De Principilis, in which he writes of the "first principles" of the creation, both earthly and heavenly. In Book II, xi, he proposes the idea of Paradise as "a place of instruction and, so to speak, a lecture room or school for souls, in which they may be taught about all that they had seen on earth and may also receive some indications of what is to follow in the future."[2] Origen combined in his thinking the Pythagorean concept of the spheres and the Christian concept of Heaven in a manner that became especially important later for Milton.[3] Of the spheres, Origen wrote:

> If anyone is ['pure in heart'] and of unpolluted mind and well-trained understanding he will make swifter progress and quickly ascend to the region of the air, until he reaches the kingdom of the heavens, passing through the series of those 'abiding places', if I may so call them, which the Greeks have termed spheres, that is, globes, but which the divine scripture calls heavens. In each of these he will first observe all that happens there, and then learn the reason why it happens; and thus he will proceed in order through each stage, following him who has 'entered into the heavens, Jesus the Son of God,' and who has said, 'I will that, where I am, they also may be with me'. Further, he alludes to this diversity of places when he says, 'in my Father's house are many abiding-places.'[4]

In the spheres, he says, the souls will learn the secrets of the universe and approach perfection. Origen, throughout his works, regards the spheres as different levels of the heavens through which the soul passes on its way to perfection. He proposes that

> when the fashion of those things which are seen passes away and all their corruptible nature has been banished and purified, and the entire condition of the world we know, in which the spheres of the planets are said to be, is left behind and superseded, there exists above that sphere which is called 'fixed' and abiding place for the pious and blessed, in as it were a 'good land' and a 'land of the living', which the 'meek' and gentle will receive for an inheritance.[5]

As M. J. Denis points out, Origen founded much of his thinking on a combination of Stoicism and Platonism, employing the hypothese and language of philosophy to clothe ideas half Christian and half Oriental, much as St. Thomas Aquinas was later to use the language of the peripatetics about substance and accident to explain the mysteries.[6]

In the third century, an asceticism developed that placed an increasing emphasis upon self-purification to enable the soul to regain what it had lost when it entered the body. This Neo-Pythagorean and Neoplatonic theosophy reached a high point with Plotinus, a Coptic Egyptian of the Alexandrian school. Both he and Origen were pupils of Ammonius Saccas, a Christian who became pagan. The Enneads of Plotinus, edited after his death by Porphyry, represent his efforts to express the reality of Soul and the only apparent reality of Body.[7] Plotinus says that "the celestial Soul—and our souls with it—springs directly next from the Creator, while the animal life of this earth is produced by an image which goes forth from that celestial Soul and may be said to flow downwards from it."[8] Soul and Body, says Plotinus, coexist in the same place: "Two bodies (i.e. by hypothesis, the Soul and the human body) are blended, each entire through the entirety of the other; where one is, the other is also; each occupies an equal extension and each the whole extension; no increase of size has been caused by the juncture: the one body thus inblended can have left the other nothing undivided."[9] With this background, we have a clearer conception of his meaning of his "mental picture of our universe":

> Each member shall remain what it is, distinctly apart; yet all is to form, as far as possible, a complete unity so that whatever comes into view, say the outer orb of the heavens, shall bring immediately with it the vision, on the one plane, of the sun and of all the stars with earth and sea and all living things as if exhibited upon a transparent globe. . . . Keep this sphere before you, and from it imagine another, a sphere stripped of magnitude and of spatial differences; cast out your inborn sense of Matter, taking care not merely to attenuate it; call on God, maker of the sphere whose image you now hold, and pray Him to

> enter. And may He come bringing His own Universe with
> all the gods that dwell in it--He who is the one God and
> all the gods, where each is all, blending into a unity,
> distinct in powers but all one god in virtue of that one
> divine power of many facets.[10]

This is what Plotinus calls multiple unity, the essence of intellectual
beauty. "We ourselves possess beauty when we are true to our own being;
our ugliness is in going over to another order; our self-knowledge, that
is to say, is our beauty; in self-ignorance we are ugly."[11] All of this is
described by Plotinus as "ordered coherence," without beginning or ending,
either spatial or temporal. It seems to go beyond a concept of harmony in
his thinking, for there is no outer compulsion involved in it. The
movement is circular. Nevertheless, much of what came to be considered
Neoplatonic came to the Renaissance through Plotinus, and his thinking
colored many of its aspects.

It is perplexing to think that Boethius (sixth century), whose
name was so familiar to Dante, Chaucer, and most others of the Middle Ages
and Renaissance, whose works on arithmetic and music were standard texts in
the schools, and who was regarded as a martyr, is seldom a familiar figure
to modern readers. Current publications of his work, especially in translation, are commonly limited to the Consolation of Philosophy; but his
De Institutione Arithmetica and De Institutione Musica were taught in many
of the great cathedral schools such as those at Rheims and Chartres. His
methods of thought began with those of the Neoplatonists, but went beyond
theirs. As Howard Rollin Patch expresses it, "the Neoplatonists led men
to the worship of intellect; Boethius brought them to God."[12] He drew upon
thinkers before him, but he was not a mere encyclopedist. He built upon
their foundations a superstructure of his own. He disagreed with Stoicism
in several respects, especially with regard to the "tabula rasa" conception
of the mind (see Book V, Poem 4, the Consolation) and the fatalism,
materialism, and pantheism expressed by the Stoics. In some other respects,
he agreed with them, especially with regard to the idea that all men are

children of one Father, God. Poem 6 of Book III, for example, expresses
exactly this idea:

> *Omne hominum genus in terris simile surgit ab ortu.*
> *Vnus enim rerum pater est, unus cunctu ministrat.*
> *Ille dedit Phoebo redios dedit et cornua lunae,*
> *Ille homines etiam terris dedit ut sidera caelo.*
> *Hic clausit membris animos celsa side petitos.*
> *Mortales igitur cunctos edit nobile germen.*
> *Quid genus et proauos strepitis? Si primordia uestra*
> *Auctoremque deum spectes, nuilus degener exstat,*
> *Ni uitiis peiora fouens proprium deserat ortum.*[13]

All, then, must partake of the harmony of the universe; and man must look
upward toward the skies, for his soul is of heaven, and he is brother to the
stars. The same father gave the sun its rays and the moon its horn, gave men
earth and the stars the sky, and clothed souls in bodies. Since all mortals
come from one noble seed, why should anyone boast of his birth and ancestors?
No one is unworthy unless he defaces his own birth with foul vice.

The concepts of earth as but a small point in the center of the
universe with only a small portion of it inhabited were already familiar,
of course, and Boethius in Book II of the Consolation of Philosophy repeated
them along with the concomitant ideas of the fickleness of earthly fame and
the harmony among the parts of the universe. This reiteration, of course,
served to make all of these concepts more and more pervasive in the
literature to come. One of Boethius' most comprehensive statements of the
concept of heavenly harmony as the mutual working for the good of all is
contained in Book IV, Poem 6, given here only in part because of its length:

> *Si uis celsi lura tonantis*
> *Pura sollers cernere mente,*
> *Aspice summi culmina caeli.*
> *Illic iusto foedere rerum*
> *Veterem seruant sidera pacem.*
> *Non sol rutilo concitus igne*
> *Gelidum Phoebus impedit axem*
> *Nec quae summo uertice mundi*
> *Flectit rapidos Vrsa meatus.*
> *Numquam occiduo iota profund*

Cetera cernens sidera mergi
Cupit oceano tingere flammas.
Semper uicibus temporis aequis
Vesper seras nuntiat umbras
Reuehitque diem Lucifer almum.
Sic aeternos reficit cursus
Alternus amor, sic astrigeris
Bellum discors exulat oris.
Haec concordia temperat aequis
Elementa modis, ut pugnantia
Vicibus cedant umida siccis
Iungantque fidem frigora flammis
Pendulus ignis surgat in altum
Terraeque graues pondere sidant.

. . . .

The harmony is exhibited in the seasons of the year and the lives of creatures on earth in their cycles. When they die, they return to their Creator who holds the reins of the world. Some things he must retard when they glide too swiftly away

Sistit retrahens ac uaga firmat.
Nam nisi rectos reuocans itus
Flexos iterum cogat in orbes,
Quae nunc stabilis continet ordo
Dissaepta suo fonte fatiscant.
Hic est cunctis commis amor
Repetuntque boni fine teneri,
Quia non aliter durare queant,
Nisi conuerso rursus amore [14]
Refluant causae quae dedit esse.

The last five lines appear to have cast their influence into the nineteenth century and Gerard Manley Hopkins' lines, in "The Leaden Echo and the Golden Echo,"

How to keep--is there any any, is there none such,
    nowhere known some, bow or brooch or braid or
    brace, lace, latch or catch or key to keep
Back beauty, keep it, beauty, beauty, beauty, . . .
    from vanishing away?
. . . .
Give beauty back, beauty, beauty, beauty, back to
    God, beauty's self and beauty's giver. [15]
. . . .

Especially pertinent to the present study is Boethius's treatise,
De Institutione Musica.[16] It and its companion, De Institutione Arithmetica,
were standard texts in schools throughout the Middle Ages and well into the
Renaissance when music was part of the Quadrivium with other sciences.
Boethius' concern with music has little to do with its enjoyment as an art
but rather with its scientific analysis and its philosophic implications.
De Musica, to use the more familiar title, is organized in two books, the
first containing thirty-three sections or chapters, some consisting of several
pages, others only a single paragraph, and the second containing thirty-one
sections. The first two chapters especially are concerned with the nature of
music as an expression of the harmony of the universe and its effect upon man.
In the Proem to Book I, he tells us that music has the natural function in
conjunction with man's conduct either to build or to destroy. It can
stimulate man's animal nature or his intelligence. According to its modes,
it can incline a listener to various types of behavior. Boethius
recapitulates here much that Plato puts forth in the Republic. In the second
chapter of Book I, Boethius divides music into three parts or types: "Et prima
quidem mundana est, secunda vero humana, tertia, quae in quibusdam constitute
est instrumentis, ut in cithara vei tibiis ceterisque, quae cantilenae
famulantur."[17] He then proceeds to discuss these three kinds.[18] The first,
musica mundana, is expressed in the heavens—that is, in the harmony of the
spheres, or in the relationships among the elements (i.e., earth, water, air,
and fire), or in the variations of the seasons or times. How, he asks, would
it be possible for the "machine of heaven" ("caeli machina") to move quickly
and also silently? The sound is not perceived by our ears, for several
reasons; but it cannot be that so swift a movement of such great bodies
should produce no tone at all, because the courses of the stars are bound
together so equally and appropriately that one is unable to comprehend it.
Some are higher, some lower; but through uniformity of motion the differences
in their courses produce order. Boethius' concept here is one aspect of the
principle of concordia discors, the harmony of disparate entities, which

plays a major part throughout Mediaeval and Renaissance thought. If, says
Boethius, harmony did not unite the diversities and contrary powers of the
four elements, how could they exist in one body and machine? It is this
diversity itself that makes it possible for the variety of seasons to produce
the body of the year. A tone that is too low or too high does not sound.
Strings stretched to too tight a tension will snap. So, too, in the universe,
nothing can be so great that its magnitude destroys something else. Every
facet of creation, then either produces its own fruit or helps others to
produce theirs. What winter confines, spring loosens, summer dries, autumn
ripens.

The second kind of music, musica humana, or "human music," everyone
sees if he looks within himself; for it is by this harmony and tempering of
deep and high voices that the body and the immaterial animation of reason are
mingled. And it is this that, as Aristotle says, joins the rational and
irrational as parts of one soul. The third type is instrumental music,
produced by means of strings, wind instruments (tibiis--pipes, flute, etc.,
originally made from a hollow tibia or other bone), or percussion. In
succeeding chapters, Boethius develops the principles of consonant tones,
proportions, the limits of human voices, the relations among the various
intervals, and other matters that go beyond the scope of our discussion,
although they can be seen as related to the theories of astronomy,
particularly to those of Kepler much later.

The influence of Boethius was great for many centuries. The
techniques of mystical vision and of contemplation were pre-eminent in
devotional instructions throughout the sixteenth and seventeenth centuries,
and emphasis was frequently placed upon man's relation with the harmony of
the universe as expressed in the Harmony of the Spheres as a specific theme.
So much was written on this theme that only a few works can be mentioned
here and recommended for further reading. Pierre Courcelle's comprehensive
and well illustrated study, La Consolation de Philosophie dans la Traditione
Littéraire,[19] in which the influence of Boethius is seen in the development

of contemplation, is especially noteworthy. The cosmic vision of St. Benoit related by Gregory the Great in the sixth century; the Mediaeval and Renaissance accounts of the visions of Jacob, Abraham, and other Biblical figures; the writings of St. Jerome, St. Augustine, and others of the early Christian church, all show the influence of the same tradition Boethius followed, or were influenced by him.

Between the sixth and eleventh centuries there appears to have been a hiatus in the development of the contemplative life. But by the twelfth century, these traditions were well established in the religious communities of Britain and northern Europe. Honorius of Autun, a Benedictine monk of Regensburg, in 1122 wrote A Picture of the World, consisting of a variety of concepts concerning the composition of the universe, including comments on the Harmony of the Spheres. He begins that section of his treatise with an orthodox statement that duplicates those found in a long succession of writings from Plato or before: "Delightful music is produced by these seven spheres revolving in sweet harmony, but tremendous though it be, we hear it not, for our ears are not attuned to it and it originates beyond the atmosphere. The only sounds that we can hear however, are such as occur in the atmosphere."[20] He gives the intervals between planets in a manner that follows sources that have been discussed earlier. He adds the information that "a tone consists of 15,625 miles; a halftone of 7,812 ½ miles. Altogether the tones add up to seven. The reason the philosophers have distinguished nine Muses is because they discovered nine consonances between earth and heaven, consonances which are implanted by nature in man."[21] But there are seven tones in our world, he says, seven tones in our music, and "the human composite represents a sevenfold blend. The body is a harmony of the four elements; the soul, of three powers; and nature has brought them together through the art of music. This is why man is called a microcosm, or smaller world, when he is thus recognized to be numerically in tune with the music of the spheres."[22] The blending here of the concepts of harmony, numerology, and man as a microcosm is of real interest and importance for the

Mediaeval and Renaissance literature to come in later years.

In the Abbey of St. Victor, just outside Paris, a congregation developed that became famous for the scholars, poets, mystics, and theologians who gathered there. Important among them were Hugo of St. Victor, a German, and Richard of St. Victor, a Scot who was born in 1123. Richard developed the ideas of Boethius concerning the three types of music along contemplative lines in which he also employed the views of Isidor of Seville and earlier philosophers. The _Tractatus de Musica_ of Hieronymus de Moravia embodies many of the concepts developed or restated by Richard.[23] Music, Richard says, occurs in, and has its effect in, a multiplicity of aspects. It is the vivifying and motivating force of all life, the first rationale and final cause of all bodies under God. For him, music appears to be the germ or nucleus of the soul and the means by which the soul reaches out to God in contemplation. The celestial ascent of Alexander the Great is pertinent to us here because of its influence on later works. The Alexander Romance of tales emerged, many half true but embellished, others wholly fanciful, still others allegorical. In some instances, there have been those who found it difficult to differentiate among them. The opening verses of I Maccabees recount the culmination of Alexander's conquest of the earth and tells us that when his kingdom was divided at his death, one of the successors was Antiochus. In much early literature Antiochus is considered a personification of the devil. Some of the romances that developed about Alexander himself present their hero, too, as Satanic because he was the predecessor of Antiochus. Alexander's successes in conquest came to be viewed as the result of God's using him as a scourge, not as the result of any virtue of Alexander's own.[24] The celestial journey comes, however, from Alexander's own supposed desire to find new lands to conquer by ascending high enough to find a wider view of the earth. The Middle English _Prose Life of Alexander_ (Thornton Manuscript) contains one version of the story:

> Thanne removed þay fra thethyn and went ay endlande þe See
> to-warde þe solstice of wynter trauellande xl days; and at þe

þay come to a reede See, and þare þay lugede bam. Ðare was faste
by a Mountayne wonder hye, One þe whilke Alexander went vp. And
when he was abown on þe heghte þare-offe, hym thoghte þat he was
nerre þe Firmament þan þe erthe; þan he ymagned in his hert swilk
a gynn how he myghte make grippes bere hym vp in-to þe ayere.
And onane he come doune of þe Mountayne and garte come bi-fore
hym his Maistre wrightes and comandid þam þat þay sulde make hym
a chayer and trelesse it wit barre of Iren one ilk a syde so þat
he my te sauely sitt bare-in. And þan he gart grynge foure
gripes and tye þam fast wit Iren cheynes vn-to þe chayere, and
in þe ouermare party of þe chayere he gart putt mete for þe
grippes. And þan he wente and sett hym in þe chayere. And
onane þe grippes bare hym vp in þe ayer so hye þat Alexander
thoghte all þe erthe na mare þan a flure þare men thressche
corne, and þe See lyke a dragon abowte þe erthe. Ðan sodaynly
a specyall vertu of godd vmbilapped þe grippes þat gart þam
discende doune to þe erthe in a felde: ten .x. day iournee fra
þe Oste, and he hadd na hurt ne na schathe in þe chayere. Bot
wit grete disesse at þe last he come till his oste.[25]

Unlike Plato's Er and Cicero's Scipio, Alexander is generally
characterized, not as a good man who ascended the Milky Way, heard the
Harmony of the Spheres, and gained insight into the ways of God and man,
but as an Antichrist whose overwhelming pride led him to attempt one more
conquest: Heaven itself. This is prevalent in the German versions, which
accounts of Alexander's celestial journey have given rise to a number of
illustrations--tapestries, mosaics, etc.--in German churches especially,
showing Alexander being borne aloft by the griffons. In History Bible I and
the Weltchronik of Enikel, it is said that when Alexander had ascended to a
certain height, a voice told him he could go no further because he had not
deserved the right through his good works. In the Middle English version
quoted above, the virtuous power of God simply dropped him in a field with
a long walk home. Basic to the German versions in many respects is the
earlier Latin Iter ad Paradisum, but it presents the legend in a different
light, wherein Alexander accepts the Wunderstein (or Philosopher's Stone)
from his aged guide, listens to him, and is reformed in his way of life.

Lydgate, in The Fall of Princes, taken from Boccaccio's De Casibus

Illustrium Vivorum, tells of Alexander's growing pride and desire to be
called a god, the son of Jupiter:

> Thoruh al his apleis & his roial halle
> A lawe he sette, upon peyne of lyff,
> That men of custom sholde hym name   calle
> This worldis monarke, nat mortal nor passiff,
> Sone to Iubiter for a prerogatyff,
> Which hadde the erthe, as god most of puissaunce,
> Conquered bi swerd onto his obeissaunce.
> (IV. 1233-1239)[26]

Calisthenes is said to have been executed for his attempt to
dissuade Alexander from this step. Interestingly, Lydgate repeats the story
of Alexander's attempts again and again to be called the son of Jupiter.
Following the account of the cutting of the Gordian knot and the defeat of
Darius, Lydgate recounts that Alexander visited the temple of Jupiter,
claiming descent from the god, "bor[e]n to been his hair, / As lord of
heuene, fir, water, erthe & hair" (1875-1876). He bribed the priests to
deify him. After Alexander had completed his conquests, says Lydgate,

> He lik a god, most pompous & elat,
> As souereyn prince of al this myddelerd,
> To take upon hym was nothyng afferd
> To cleyme in contres, a thyng that was not fair,
> Of Iubiter to be bothe sone & hair.
> (2145-2149)

It is small wonder that the view of Alexander's pride became a part of the
tradition surrounding him. In the geocentric universe, pride became viewed
more and more as a vice, and, indeed, as the vice underlying all others. For
Pre-Christian society, it was faulty reasoning to accord too much pride in
man's place in the scale of creatures. For the Christian, it became a sin to
do so, for it made the center of the universe seem of more worth than the
outermost sphere, whereas the truth lay in the opposite direction. Humility
in the centricity of earth and man was the key to the ascent of the soul to
the outermost sphere, the sphere where the key to harmony was to be found.

NOTES

[1] Boethius, The Consolation of Philosophy, trans., Richard Green (New York: Bobbs-Merrill Company The Library of Liberal Arts , 1962), p. 76, This edition of the Consolation of Philosophy is hereafter cited as the LLA edition.

[2] Origen, On First Principles, trans. from Koetschau's Text by G. W. Butterworth (New York: Harper and Row [Torchbooks, The Cathedral Library], 1966), p. 152.

[3] Paradise Lost, VIII, p. 98-106.

[4] Origen, p. 152

[5] Origen, II. iii, p. 93.

[6] M. J. Denis, De La Philosophie D'Origene (Paris: L'Imprimerie Nationale, 1884), p. 60. The reader is also referred to an extensive discussion of Origen's eclecticism with respect to Platonism and theology in Zur Theologie des Biblischen Wortes bei Origenes by Rolf Gogler (Dusseldorf: Patmos-Verlag, 1963), Chapter IV.

[7] A readable and comprehensive discussion of the character of Plotinus' thought is presented by Will Durant in Caesar and Christ (New York: Simon and Schuster, 1944), pp. 607-611.

[8] Plotinus, The Enneads, trans., Stephen MacKenna, 2nd ed. revised by B. S. Page, Second Ennead, I, "The Heavenly System" (London: Faber and Faber, 1956), p. 83.

[9] Ibid., IV. 8, p. 350.

[10] Plotinus, V. 8, p. 429.

[11] Ibid., p. 433.

[12] Howard Rollin Patch, The Tradition of Beothius (New York: Oxford University Press, 1935), p. 5.

[13]Consolation of Philosophy, III, Poem 6, in Boethius, The Theological Tractates, trans., H. F. Stewart and E. K. Rand; The Consolation of Philosophy, trans. H. F. Stewart (New York: G. P. Putnam's Sons [Loeb Library], 1926), pp. 248-250.

All quotations from the Tractates or the Consolation of Philosophy from this edition are hereafter cited as Loeb edition.

[14]Loeb edition, pp. 352-356

[15]Gerard Manley Hopkins, Poems and Prose, ed., W. H. Garnder (Baltimore: Penguin Books, 1953), pp. 52-54.

[16]Anicii Manlil Torquati Severini Boetil, De Institutione Arithmetica, De Institutione Musica, ed., Godofredus Friedlein (Leipzig: Minerva G.M.B.H., 1966). All references to De Musica are to this edition, hereafter cited as De Musica.

[17]De Musica, I. ii, p. 187.

[18]Ibid., I. ii, pp. 187-189. I here present the substance of Boethius' discussion but do not translate literally at all points.

[19]Pierre Courcelle, La Consolation de Philosophie dans la Traditione Litteraire: Antecedents et Posterite de Boece (Paris: Etudes Augustiniennes, 1967).

[20]Honorius of Autun, "A Picture of the World," in Medieval Philosophy: from St. Augustine to Nicholas of Cusa, ed., John F. Wippel (New York: The Free Press, 1969), p. 183.

[21]Ibid.

[22]"A Picture of the World," pp. 183-184.

[23]Hieronymus de Moravia, O. P., Tractatus de Musica, ed., Dr. Simon M. Cserba (Regensburg: Friedrich Pustet, 1935).

[24]George Cary, The Medieval Alexander (Cambridge: The University

Press, 1956), pp. 121-127 passim.

[25]<u>The Prose Life of Alexander: from the Thornton MS</u>., ed., J. S.
Westlake (London: Kegan Paul [Early English Text Society], 1913 [for 1911]),
pp. 105-106.

[26]<u>Lydgate's Fall of Princes</u>, ed., Henry Bergen, Part II (Oxford:
Oxford Univ. Press for Early English Text Society, 1924), p. 507.

CHAPTER III

CHAUCER AND THE DREAM OF HARMONY

O Thought, that wrot al that I mette,
And in the tresorye hyt shette
Of my brayn, now shal men se
Yf any vertu in the be,
To tellen al my drem aryght.
Now kythe thyn engyn and myght!
                    (The House of Fame II, 523-528)[1]

Chaucer opens the second part of The House of Fame by invoking one
of the most essential attributes of one who would gain the spiritual vision
that is implicit in the idea of universal harmony--clearness of thought, the
virtue to recount clearly the story of his celestial journey for the benefit
of "every maner man / That Englissh understonde kan" (509-510).

The House of Fame presents probably the earliest evidence of
Chaucer's concern with the concept of the celestial dream journey in search
of the nature of harmony. F. N. Robinson places it in Chaucer's period of
"transitional works, partly of the French tradition, but showing the
beginnings of Italian influence," dating between 1372 and 1380.[2] We can
expect, then, to find in it a measure of Chaucer's growing knowledge of the
works of such representatives of the Italian literary heritage as Boethius,
Dante, Petrarch, and Boccaccio, and their classical predecessors. In the
Proem, Chaucer draws upon the Mediaeval concepts concerning dreams and
describes the state of confusion and frustration to which a man of his time
might well be subject with the variety of theories concerning cause, types of
dreams, interpretations, and emotional effects of the "dream" or "sweven,"
the "avisioun" or the "revelacioun" that might invade sleep. "God turne

39

us every drem to goode!" he begins in the first line. Macrobius classifies
dreams under five main types,[3] and then says that "the dream which Scipio
reports that he saw embraces the three reliable types i.e., not a nightmare
or apparition . . . and also has to do with all five varieties of the
enigmatic dream," by which he means "one that conceals with strange shapes
and veils with ambiguity the true meaning of the information being offered,
and requires an interpretation for its understanding."[4] In the enigmatic
dream the dreamer is accompanied on a celestial journey by a guide who shows
him wonders and tells him great truths from which he learns the secrets of
the universe and of life.

The dream related by Chaucer in The House of Fame takes place on
the tenth of December. Scipio related his dream during a winter festival;
and, although he does not tell us the date of the dream itself, the relationship in Chaucer's thinking appears possible. B. G. Koonce reminds us, in his
study of Chaucer and the Tradition of Fame, that "dates are similarly attached
to visions of prophetic significance."[5] He cites the Old Testament books of
Ezekiel, Daniel, and Zechariah in particular. Prophetic visions were considered to be brought about by the influence of God upon the intelligences
that direct the planets. Before the fall of man, all of these were ex-
pressive of harmony; but afterward, when the harmony had been disrupted, evil
influences were thought to have come into play as well.[6] Chaucer dates his
dream on December tenth. The tenth day of the tenth month, the Biblical
equivalent of December tenth, was the date of the beginning of the siege of
Jerusalem by Nebuchadnezzar, according to the record in 2 Kings 25:1: "And
in the ninth year of his reign, in the tenth month, on the tenth day of the
month, Nebuchadnezzar king of Babylon came with all his army against
Jerusalem, and laid siege to it." Allegorically, the siege of Jerusalem
signifies the siege of the Church by the forces of the world; and
Nebuchadnezzar becomes Satan. Jerusalem also represents the soul of man
besieged by Sin. For St. Jerome, the tenth day of the tenth month prefigures
Doomesday.[7] If Chaucer intended to make allegorical significations in any

or all of these terms, the poem may then take on further meanings of temporal and eternal values. We recall also that in Book I Chaucer is much concerned with Troy, another besieged city.

The tenth of December can also be given astrological significance, which of course cannot be disregarded with respect to mediaeval writers. Koonce points out that on that date the sun is in the sign of Sagittarius, the house of Jupiter, which is in the ninth of the twelve houses of the zodiac and "is assigned special attributes or 'influences' that have acquired value as Christian symbols. As distinguished from the others, the ninth house is the house of faith and religion, and its powers, we are told, are exerted especially in such spiritual matters as prophetic dreams, pilgrimages, and heavenly tidings."[8] Jupiter is also credited by such writers as Roger Bacon and Pierre Bersuire with benevolence and love and is even sometimes equated with the goodness of Christ.[9]

Dante, in Purgatorio VI, invokes Jove, or Jupiter, in the context of Christ:

E se licito m'e, o sommo Giove,
Che fosti in terra per noi crucifisso,
Son il giusti occhi tuoi rivolti altrove?
O e preparazion, che ne l'abisso
Dei tuo consiglio fai, per alcun bene
In tutto de l'accorger nostro scisso?
(Purgatorio VI. 118-123)[10]

Does the highest Jove, crucified on earth for our sins, turn his just eyes away from us? Or is he preparing a plan, good in his sight but hidden from us?

Chaucer's close following of many of Dante's symbols and allusions is emphasized, then, in his choice of a date that places his dream under the influence exerted by Jove over prophetic dreams in particular. December tenth has a strong liturgical significance as well as Koonce points out. It comes during Advent, a time of joy in the coming of Christ and of somberness in its implied anticipation of His second coming. Also, in astronomical tables the position of the sun on December tenth counteracts the malevolent tendencies of Mars and Saturn, especially the latter. The position of Saturn, in this context and during Advent, signifies time and man's adversity under the old law before the coming of Christ. Saturn's attributes of coldness and dryness then come to signify "frigidity and sterility of the spirit and its captivity by sin."[11] Therefore, the presence of Saturn in the ninth house--the house of journeys and pilgrimages--must be counteracted by the sun and Jupiter in order to prevent disaster to one making the celestial journey. This favorable condition exists on December tenth, and it exists during day and night alike. Chaucer, then, addresses his Invocation "with special devocion / Unto the god of slep anon" (68-69) in order that his dreams be true and not misleading; and to this god of sleep, he adds,

> Prey I that he wol me spede
> My sweven for to telle aryght,
> Yf every drem stonde in his myght.
>
> (78-80)

The tales of false love that follow are learned in Venus' temple of glass, but the dreamer does not know "ne where I am, ne in what contree," (I-474) and must

> . . . goo out and see,
> Ryght at the wiket, yf y kan
> Se owhere any stiryng man,
> That may me telle where I am.
>
> (475-479)

Here he finds himself in a large field that immediately reminds us of the vision of Er. What has gone before can be seen as preludial to the true vision to follow. What he has seen so far is of Venus and is concerned with the falseness of earthly and merely courtly love.

In La Vita Nuova, Dante has made a similar transition. In this early collection of prose and sonnets, his first work, Dante makes the transition from the romantic love in the manner of the troubadours of Provence in which Amor is central to the poet's grief for his dead Beatrice to a new vision in which Beatrice is herself Love. Charles S. Singleton explains,

>   The disappearance of the God of Love from the Vita Nuova
> is nothing less than a deliberate removal. That removal,
> however, is all in the way of recantation of troubadour love
> which the Vita Nuova makes. The God of Love is, indeed, the
> veriest sign and symbol of such love. But if this is recantation,
> it is very unlike the traditional kind, because even if the God
> is abolished, love of woman is not abandoned. Beatrice remains.
> In fact, the whole authority of Love is transferred to her.
> Beatrice is Love. And Beatrice remains to the end. Yet,
> between love of her and love of God there is no conflict. When
> the Vita Nuova ends, it faces God; but it keeps Beatrice.[12]

It is a progression from Amor to Caritas, from the old life of troubadour
love for the beautiful Beatrice to the new life of "disinterested love having
its final perfection in Heaven."[13] The progression, then, from one point to
another of both of these dream visions--La Vita Nuova and The House of Fame--
is from earthly to heavenly love, from false to true vision. Chaucer, coming
out of Venus' "temple ymad of glas" (I, 120), and finding himself in the
desert field, immediately seeks the truth. He looks up and prays for Christ
to protect him from hallucination and sees

>   . . . an egle sore,
> But that hit semed moche more
> Then I had any egle seyn.
> But this as sooth as deth, certeyn,
> Hyt was of gold, and shon so bryghte
> That never sawe men such a syghte,
> But yf the heven had ywonne
> Al newe of gold another sonne;
> So shone the egles fethers bryghte,
> And somwhat dounward gan hyt lyghte.
>   (499-509)

In the field the dreamer goes through a transition to the true dream, the
celestial journey, the dream of revelation; and the eagle becomes the guide
whereby this transition is achieved.

     Dante has done much the same thing in the Purgatorio. Earlier
dreaming has been of events and people of old. Then comes a change, both of

time and of dream. Canto IX opens,

> La concubina di Titone antico,
>   Gia s'imbiancava al balco d' oriente,
>   Fuor de le braccia del suo doice amico;
>   (Purgatorio IX, 1-3)

The moon is the concubine of old Tithonus, since Aurora is his true spouse.
Also, the rising of the moon is a false dawn.[14]

For Chaucer as for Dante, the field is the site of the appearance
of the golden eagle. For Dante the eagle appears as a figment of the
meditating mind, appearing when the mind is wandering in contemplation, "a
le sue vision quasi e divina" (Purgatorio IX, 18), and swoops to the same
field from which Ganymede had been snatched. Chaucer's eagle descends to a
field

> Withouten toun, or hous, or tree,
> Or bush, or grass, or eryd lond;
> For al the feld nas but of sond
> As smal as man may se yet lye
> In the desert of Lybye.
>   (House of Fame I, 484-488)

Chaucer the dreamer differs in an important aspect from most
personas who have made the celestial journey. Scipio's ascent came after an
evening of talk with an old friend while he was engaged in an expedition of
conquest, Pompey's and Er's after death in battle. But Chaucer has been
reading. In fact, says his guide, the golden Eagle, that is all he had done.
He writes of love and life, but he knows either only from books:

> . . . thou hast no tydynges
> Of Loves folk yf they be glade,
> Ne of noght elies that God made;
> And noght oonly fro fer contree
> That ther no tydynge cometh to thee,
> But of thy verray neyghebores,
> That duellen almost at thy dores,
> Thou herist neyther that ne this;
> For when thy labour doon al ys,
> And hast mad alle thy rekenynges,

In stede of reste and newe thynges,
Thou goost hom to thy hous anoon;
And, also domb as any stoon,
Thou sittest at another book
Tyl fully daswed ys thy look,
And lyvest thus as an here myte,
Although thyn abstynence ys lyte.

(House of Fame II, 644–660)

Kemp Malone says that the temple of Venus and the barren sandy field "may be taken, then to stand for the literary life Chaucer was leading before the eagle carried him off: composing courtly-love poems and reading books."[15] Chaucer the dreamer needs to gain perspective; but it is not the perspective of humility, of seeing the smallness of earth in the hugeness of the universe. It is, rather, the perspective of life rather than a vicarious knowledge about life and a view of true love rather than courtly love. He must be taken, therefore, by the eagle,

. . . in his clawes starke
As lyghtly as I were a larke,
How high, I can not telle yow,
For I cam up, y nyste how
(II. 545–548)

to the place where he can hear all that happens and witness the results of men's real actions.

The eagle itself, of course, is a frequent symbol of clearness of vision, both physical and spiritual. A twelfth century Bestiary tells us that "Aquila the Eagle is called so from the acuteness (acumine) of his eyes," but that when his vision becomes darkened,

he goes in search of a fountain, and, over against it, he flies up to the height of heaven, even unto the circle of the sun; and there he singes his wings and at the same time evaporates the fog of his eyes, in a ray of the sun. Then at length, taking a header down into the fountain, he dips himself three times in it, and instantly he is renewed with a great vigour of plumage and splendour of vision.

> Do the same thing, O Man, you who are clothed in the old
> garment and have the eyes of your heart growing foggy. Seek
> for the spiritual fountain of the Lord and lift up your mind's
> eye to God--who is the fount of justice--and then your mouth
> will be renewed like the eagle's. 16

The eagle seems a fitting guide for one whose vision of life has become
clouded. We recall here the ascent of Alexander whose chariot was borne
by four griffons. The eagle mentioned in the Bible is said to be "the
griffon (Gyps fulvus), or great vulture, a bird very abundant in Palestine
and adjacent countries. . . . [much nobler than a vulture and used by
Orientals] as the type of the lordly and great."[17] The griffon described by
Philip Schaff has an eight-foot wingspread, so would not be implausible as
a means of transportation. Sir Humphry Davy describes its flight as an
ascending spiral toward the sun.[18] But it may also be noted that Dante's
and Chaucer's golden eagles need no instigation to flight other than the
inspiration to rise toward the physical and spiritual sun, whereas Alexander's
four griffons had to be enticed upward trying to reach ever-unattainable
pieces of meat mounted on pikes above their heads.

Koonce describes the House of Fame as possessing in its structure
much the same format as that employed by Dante in the Divine Comedy, and we
have already seen some evidence of that. Both are set forth as dream
journeys, of course; and Koonce equates the three parts into which each is
divided: "the desert of Venus in Book I [of the House of Fame], the flight of
Jupiter's eagle in Book II, and the mountain of Fame in Book III, paralleling
the 'gran diserto' of Hell, the flight of the golden eagle of Purgatory, and
the purgatorial mountain whose ascent leads to the beatific vision of
Paradise."[19]

Book II has been mentioned most often for the way in which Chaucer
has established his eagle as a comic character who is perturbed by the
nervousness of his passenger, whose heart is thumping aloud:

. . . 'Seynte Marye!

Thou art noyous for to carye,
And nothyng nedeth it, pardee!
For, also wis God helpe me,
As thou noon harm shalt have of this.
                    (II. 573-577)

He is the erudite messenger of Jove whose mission is to acquaint "Geffrey"
with the nature of the universe and its parts. Chaucer, as has already been
mentioned, has been chosen for this journey, not because he has attained
great clarity of insight, but because he needs to be helped to gain it. The
eagle is an enthusiastic teacher, and his love is to impart knowledge. What
better opportunity can he find than this. The House of Fame, to which the
eagle is taking the dreamer, has an abundance of everything he wishes to
show his pupil; for

Hir paleys stant, as I shal seye,
Ryght even in myddes of the weye
Betwixen hevene, erthe, and see;
That what so ever in all these three
Is spoken, either privy or apert,
The way therto ys so overt,
Abd stant eke in so juste a place
That every soun mot to hyt pace,
Or what so cometh from any tonge,
Be hyt rouned, red, or songe,
Or spoke in suerte or in drede,
Certeyn, hyt moste thider nede.
                    (II. 713-724)

The chief message appears to center about the idea of orderliness, of harmony
in creation:

. . . every thyng enclyned to ys,
Hath his kyndelyche stede:
That sheweth hyt, withouten drede,
That kyndely the mansioun
Of every speche, of every soun,
Be hyt eyther foul or fair,
Hath hys kynde place in ayr.
                    (II. 828-834)

This is the realm, then, not of Fortuna but of Natura; not of fickle and

disorderly change but of natural order and growth. It is not until the eagle
has clarified this point that he tells "Geffrey" to look down and see

> "By thy trouthe, yond adoun,
> Wher that thou knowest any toun,
> Or hous, or any other thing."
> (889–891)

The dreamer, looking down, soon finds that the cities and towns, trees, hills,
and valleys are disappearing from sight; they have

> . . . flowen fro the ground so hye
> That all the world, as to myn ye,
> No more semed than a prikke.
> (905–907)

But he is still not sure that this is not merely another false dream: "Or
elles was the air so thikke / That y ne myghte not discerne" (908–909).
Others have not been half so high, the eagle assures him; and he is told to
look upward and 'se yonder, loo, the Galaxie, / Which men clepeth the Milky
Way' (936–937). They rise higher, and, Chaucer the poet is overcome with the
vision before him: "'O God!' quod y, 'that made Adam, / Moche ys thy myght
and thy noblesse!'" (970–971. He thinks of Boethius

> That writ, "A thought may flee so hye,
> Wyth fetheres of Philosophye,
> To passen everych element;
> And when he hath so fer ywent,
> Than may be seen, behynde hys bak,
> Cloude." . . .
> (973–978)

With St. Paul, he comes to be filled with wonder and ecstasy:

> Thoo gan y wexen in a were,
> And seyde, "Y wot wel y am here;
> But wher in body or in gost
> I not, ywys; but God, thou wost!"
> (979–982)

This is the second time the poet has not known where he was. But this time he is content to trust God, who does know; "for more clere entendement / Nas me never yit ysent" (983-984) and he is therefore unafraid. He turns his thoughts to those who have described the heavens, realized that they were right from what he sees now, and concludes that he can believe them.

The eagle, however, has little patience with this philosophizing and wants to get on with the astronomy lesson. "'Lat be,' quod he, 'thy fantasye! / Wilt thou lere of sterres aught?'" (992-993). But Chaucer is not interested in the scientific side of the matter. When the eagle asks him if he does not hear the great sound--in this case the rumbling of speech in the House of Fame--he replies, we infer with some asperity, "Yis, parde! . . . wel ynough" (1032). With another explanation of what the poet is to learn and a prayer that "God of heven sende the grace / Some good to lernen in this place" (1087-1088), the eagle, like Dante's Virgil, leaves. Unlike Virgil, however, the eagle does not hand Chaucer over to a new guide; there is no Beatrice in the House of Fame. The dreamer must watch and observe for himself, but the "tydynges" he finds there are not what he expected to find, he tells the anonymous "frend" after a time. The lesson of the House of Fame must come by negative example.

In Dante's third book and in Chaucer's, Apollo is invoked for aid in successful writing. Chaucer's House of Fame, however, and Dante's Paradise are not the same place despite this invocation to the same patron. The House of Fame is rather an inversion of celestial perfection. So much has been written of the mutable aspects of the place that little need be added. The reference almost at once to castles in Spain, the mount of ice and names that melt, the list of harpers and singers of whom several are those whose songs appeal to the senses and incite the listener to the love of pleasure rather than of God, the lavishness of the decoration and gems that blind the eye of the beholder, all point to the reversal of values. Koonce relates Fame to the Whore of Babylon.[20] The palace of Fame is, like that of Wisdom, supported by seven pillars; but in the palace of Fame they are pillars of writers of

the pre-Christian era. The pillars themselves are of baser metals and
"uncler," but they are also metals that symbolize various pagan deities; and
"though they nere of no rychesse, / Yet they were mad for gret noblesse"
(423-424). These, then, are seven pillars of wisdom, but wisdom of man and
of earth and therefore mutable, just as are the deeds reported by the suppli-
cants. Significantly, there is no harmony of the spheres to be heard here.
There is "hevenyssh melodye" (1395), but it is the song of Calliope, the muse
of epic poetry, and her eight sisters--Clio of history, Urania of astronomy,
Melpomene of tragedy, Thalia of comedy, Terpsichore of dance, Erato of love-
poetry, Polyhymnia of songs to the gods, and Euterpe of lyric poetry.[21]

By this time, Chaucer the dreamer has learned "where that Fame
duelled, . . . / And eke of her descripcioun" (1902-1903); but he still needs
to hear more "tydynges." J. A. W. Bennett proposes that Chaucer's need has
been for new material about which to write. The word "tydynges," he says,
"is more specific than 'talk', less literary than novella. 'Tales' alone
will serve to convey the fourteenth-century range of meaning, since it
touches on 'anecdote' or 'story' at one extreme, 'report' or 'rumour' at the
other."[22] I would go a little further than Bennett and propose that these
"tydynges" that Chaucer needs are more in the sense of "truths" or "sentence"
in the sense in which Chaucer uses that word. In the first place, "tales" he
can get from books; it is to counteract this very thing that the eagle has
brought him aloft. In the second place, it is for aid in achieving "sentence"
that he invokes Apollo at the beginning of Book III, more than craft. It was
stated by the eagle in the beginning that Chaucer was too dependent upon books,
was too introverted. He is being thrust now into a maelstrom of activity.
The new "frend" to whom he tells his thoughts leads him out of the castle,
and he sees in the valley below the wicker House of Rumor. He sees also his
first guide, the eagle, perched on a rock.

And I gan streghte to hym gon,
And seyde thus: 'Y preye the
That thou a while abide me,
For Goddis love, and lete me seen

> What wondres in this place been;
> For yit, paraunter, y may lere
> Som good thereon, or sumwhat here
> That leef me were, or that y wente.'
>   'Petre! that is myn entente,'
> Quod he to me; 'therfore y duelle. . . .'
>   (III. 1992-2001)

Once more, then, he is carried upward by the golden eagle, "betweene hys toon" (2028) and set down in the new place.

What the dreamer was to have learned at this point, we of course can only guess. The whirling house itself appears to admit of several interpretations at the same time. Chaucer tells us it is the "Domus Dedaly, / That Laboryntus cleped ys" (1920-1921); and its wicker-work structure, its lack of durability, its many apertures all point to its significance as a temporal maze of the world. Bennett reminds us of the wicker cage in which the griffons carried Alexander; and B. G. Koonce calls the House of Rumor an inversion of Solomon's temple built of strong timbers. He points out that "the image of the cage echoes the Apocalypse, where the angel of 'great authority' compares Babylon to a stronghold 'of every unclean and hateful bird' which will be destroyed at the Last Judgment."[23]

Once inside the whirling cage, the dreamer feels no sense of whirling. In the center of the universe, the turning is no longer perceptible. The cage, then, appears to be a representation of the macrocosm. As no tale is unchanged from beginning to end, so the tidings here echo and double as they go. As Bennett proposes, "the poet . . . when divinely guided, can reach the still centre of this turning world, can watch the whole process of a tale's gestation."[24] If we accept this as a plausible interpretation, Chaucer the poet has learned that which Jupiter sought to teach him—to look at life and his fellow man, to look upward and ahead rather than downward and back.

In the opening stanzas of The Parliament of Fowls, Chaucer declares again his lack of personal experience in the art of Love and at the same

time his fascination with "his wonderful werkynge" (5). Although he lacks
experience, he says, "Yit happeth me ful ofte in bokes reede / Of his
myrakles and his crewel yre" (10-11). Once again, then, as in The House of
Fame, we find the poet reiterating his dependence upon books for his knowledge about life—a device, undoubtedly, for introducing a literary source
because of either its authority, its wisdom, or its attractiveness. It is
in this poem that Chaucer deals most explicitly and most extensively with the
Somnium Scipionis of Cicero, which, as I noted in Chapter I, was then available only in the fifth century Commentarii in Somnivm Scipionis by Macrobius.[25]
In the introduction to his translation of Macrobius, William Harris Stahl
says:

> Usually Chaucer does not seem to be aware of the fact
> that Macrobius was the author of only the Commentary and that
> Scipio's Dream was the work of Cicero. In the opening lines
> of the Romaunt of the Rose Macrobius is supposed to be the
> author of the Dream and Scipio the Younger is referred to as
> 'king Cipioun.' Again in the Book of the Duchess (284-87) it is
>   Macrobeus
>   (He that wrot al th'avysyoun
>   That he mette, kyng Scipioun)
> In the House of Fame (916) Scipio is "kyng, Daun Scipio,"
> and in the Nun's Priest Tale (VII, 3123-25) Scipio's Dream is
> attributed to Macrobius. In The Parliament of Fowls, however,
> Chaucer understands that Cicero is the author of the Dream
>   Tullyus of the Dream of Scipioun (31) and that
> Macrobius wrote the Commentary
>   Of which Macrobye roughte nat a lyte (III).[26]

Therefore, it would appear that, in The Parliament of Fowls, Chaucer has
become increasingly knowledgeable about the Somnium in many respects besides
its authorship and with the Platonic principles delineated within it. A
number of scholars call our attention to Chaucer's omission of most of the
matter in the middle sections of Macrobius' commentary and infer from that
that Chaucer may not have read all of it. But Stahl reminds us that
Macrobius used the Somnium Scipionis largely as a springboard for expounding
a variety of Pythagorean and Platonic concepts. Although Chaucer does not

appear to have made much use of the more technical portions of the Commentary, this was probably a matter of selection and of suiting his own immediate audience in the English court.

The question that immediately arises with respect to The Parliament of Fowls is that of the relationship between Chaucer's opening statement of his lack of firsthand knowledge in matters of love and the subject of Scipio's dream--the ascent to the spheres and the hearing of their harmony, the discussion of the immortality of the soul, and the importance of loving justice and duty as the way to heaven. Bernard F. Huppé and D. W. Robertson, Jr., in Fruyt and Chaf, see a parallel between Chaucer's garden of love and the church as it should be, a world "which is in a very real sense a 'garden of love.'"[27] This, then, is the harmony that should be. It is the domain of Natura.

Under this system of allegory, the park with its green walls is Paradise; the walls equal Faith. Bennett remarks that for Mediaeval and some Renaissance painters, a "civilized" garden was an enclosed one. "The wall enclosed the known, the beautiful, and the ordered, shutting them off from wilderness and rough weather. Eden was the more Eden when it was 'piked with a palisade'; so Milton fences it with a 'verdurous wall.' The very word paradisus represents the Persian 'pairidaeza,' a walled enclosure."[28] The universe, too, under the system of the spheres, is enclosed, ordered, and shut off from chaos.

Chaucer's garden is not, however, an unfallen Eden in the view either of Huppé and Robertson or of Bennett. It is a post-lapsarian Eden, and that fact is intimated almost at once by Chaucer in his catalogue of trees:

> For overal where that I myne eyen caste
> Were trees clad with leves that ay shal laste
> Ech in his kynde, of colour fresh and greene
> As emeraude, that joye was to seene.   175
>
> The byldere ok, and ek the hardy asshe;

```
The piler elm, the cofre unto carayne;
The boxtre pipere, holm to whippes lashe;
The saylynge fyr; the cipresse, deth to playne;
The shetere ew; the asp for shaftes pleyne;    180
The olyve of pes, and eke the dronke vyne;
The victor palm, the laurer to devyne.
                    (172-182)
```

These are trees with eternal leaves, the trees of Eden. But they are trees
that must serve fortunate and unfortunate purposes alike. The "piler elm."
may support a vine, as Robinson suggests in a note, and it must also provide
a handle for a whip. The good and bad, fortunate and sad functions of the
trees are seen side by side, just as the dreamer found, when he first
approached the gates to which Africanus led him, that the garden of love has
two aspects. It can be a place of pleasure, "the blysful place / Of hertes
hele and dedly woundes cure" (127-128) or lead to "the mortal strokes of the
spere / Of which Disdayn and Daunger is the gyde" (135-136). Similarly, in
the Somnium Scipionis, Cicero's Africanus points out to Scipio the many
victories and successes that would be his in life "if only you escape the
wicked hands of your kinsmen,"[30] the dangers, then, of the fallen world.
Earthly fame, Scipio learns, is mutable. As he stands in the heavens and
listens to the music of the spheres, Africanus notices that he looks back at
earth: *"Sentio, inquit, te sedem etiam nunc hominum ac domum contemplari;
quae si tibi parva, ut est, ita videtur, haec caelestia semper spectato, illa
humana contemnito. Tu enim quam celebritatem sermonis hominum aut quam expe-
tendam consequi gloriam potes?"*[31] Africanus perceives, he says, that Scipio
still contemplates the domain of men. If earth looks as small to him as it
really is, he should disdain earthly matters, look only to celestial ones;
for what fame among men could he expect that would be worth striving for?

Twice in the early stanzas of The Parliament of Fowls, Chaucer
emphasizes the need for devotion to the "commune profyt," the good of all.
Both times, he does so while recounting the Somnium Scipionis:

Thanne telleth it that, from a sterry place,

> How Affrycan hath hym Cartage shewed,
> And warnede hym beforn of al his grace,
> And seyde hym what man, lered other lewed
> That lovede commune profyt, wel I thewed,
> He shulde into a blysful place wende,
> There as joye is that last withouten ende.
>
> (43-49)

The passage here referred to is to be found in sections XI to XIII, and the "commune profyt" reference is undoubtedly to the last of these, in which Africanus tells Scipio that *"omnibus, qui patriam conservaverint, adiuverint, auxerint, certum esse in caelo definitum locum, ubi beati aevo sempiterno fruantur. . . ."*[32] The phrase *"esse in caelo"* denotes heaven as the height of joy or renown[33] so that all who have preserved, supported, and aided their fatherland are assured of a definite place in the heavens for everlasting joy and renown.

The second Chaucerian reference in question is in a two-stanza passage:

> Thanne preyde hym Scipion to telle hym al
> The wey to come into that hevene lisse.
> And he seyde, "Know thyself first immortal,
> And loke ay besyly thow werche and wysse
> To commune profit, and thow shalt not mysse
> To comen swiftly to that place deere
> That ful of blysse is and of soules cleere.
>
> "But brekers of the lawe, soth to seyne,
> And likerous folk, after that they ben dede,
> Shul whirle aboute th'erthe alwey in peyne,   80
> Tyl many a world be passed, out of drede,
> And than, foryeven al hir wikked dede,
> Than shul they come into this blysful place,
> To which to comen God the sende his grace."
>
> (71-84)

Chaucer has here partially translated and condensed the last three sections of the Somnium which read in part, *"Tu vero enitere et sic habeto, non esse e mortalem, sed corpus hoc; nec enim tu is es, quem forma ista declarat, sed mens cuiusque is est quisque, non ea figura, quae digito demonstrari potest.*

. . ." and conclude, "*quae si est una ex omnibus, quae sese moveat, neque
nata certe est et aeterna est. Hanc tu exerce optimis in rebus! Sunt autem
optimae curae de salute patrie, quibus agitatus et exercitatus animus
velocius in hanc sedem et domum suam pervolabit; . . . Namque eorum animi,
que se corporis voluptatibus dediderunt earumque se quasi ministros prae-
buerunt inpulsuque libidinum voluptatibus oboedientium deorum et hominum
iura violaverunt, corporibus elapsi circum terram ipsam volutantur nec hunc
in locum nisi multis exagitati saeculis revertuntur.*"[34]

Macrobius' commentary on these passages offers extensive discussion
of the Platonic origin of the ideas. The body is only the outward form, says
Cicero here; "*sed mens cuiusque is est quisque.*" The reason, intellect,
understanding—all that go to comprise "spirit"—are everything, not the body
that can be indicated with a finger. This is shown because it is the spirit
that moves the body; and it is in turn moved by God. It has no beginning
and is eternal. Therefore, it should be used for optimum returns; and the
best of these are for the good of the fatherland. He who follows such a
goal will reach heaven quickly, but he who wastes his spirit on pleasures of
the appetite will whirl about in the lower air for many ages before he can
return to heaven. This last appears of course to be a pre-Christian concept
of what came to be called Purgatory.

Chaucer, then, in both cases has adapted Cicero's concept of the
highest good being service to the nation and referred it simply to "common
profit." It is between these two passages that Chaucer refers to the
harmony of the spheres:

> Thanne shewede he hym the lytel erthe that here is,
> At regard of the hevenes quantite;
> And after shewede he hym the nyne speres,
> And after that the melodye herde he
> That cometh of thilke speres thryes thre,
> That welle is of musik and melodye
> In this world here, and cause of armonye.
> (57-63)

Much has been made of the fact that Chaucer perhaps erred in attributing the melody to all nine spheres whereas Cicero considers seven tones, and Macrobius discusses seven as a perfect number. It does not appear so important, however, as Chaucer's intimation that all nine--including the Primum Mobile or Heaven (as first mover) and earth--are included in the harmonius relationship. The relationship among all nine parts of the universe is of greater importance to Chaucer than the technically "accurate" number. The House of Fame, he has said, lies in the midst of the three places, heaven, earth, and sea. The harmony here depends upon the relationship of "thilke speres thryes thre;" harmony results from the concern of all for the common good. Chaucer is himself deeply concerned for his own sins of omission and commission as he goes to bed and to his dream.

It is in the garden that the importance of these ideas becomes clear. Where everything serves for the common good, whether some of the functions be fortunate, sad, or merely necessary (as in the trees already mentioned), where there can be rabbits playing and also "the dredful ro" alongside "bestes smale of gentil kynde," then there can be harmony:

> Of instruments of strenges in acord
> Herde I so pleye a ravyshyng swetnesse,
> That God, that makere is of al and lord,
> Ne herde nevere beter, as I gesse.
> (197-200)

But it is a harmony threatened by danger, for Cupid and his daughter Will are there preparing their weapons. It is a garden where both spirtual delights and earthly pleasure live side by side, both peace and danger. It is a garden like the world itself, where man must make choices. Nearby is the temple of brass of Venus--but the wrongful Venus of lechery, pride, and desire. The pillars of Venus' temples are of jasper, called by Huppé and Robertson "green like the stones which make up the wall of faith" of the garden itself, but which "cannot be those of true faith, and probably represent the foolish faith of lovers who trust in earthly love."[35]

Within the temple are the inversions of the true love that cause
disharmony in the world--sin and vice, jealousy, world riches, and a list of
tragic lovers who were victims of the false Venus. It is at this point that
the dreamer approaches the hillside upon which he finds the "noble goddesse
Nature" and the assembly of birds. Unlike the birds of the garden, who sang
"with voys of aungel in here armonye" (191), these make "so huge a noyse"
(312) and create such a throng "that unether was there space / For me to
stonde, so ful was al the place" (314-315). It is St. Valentine's Day, of
course, and the confusion is brought about by the conflict between the ideal
and the earthly. Huppé and Robertson tell us that the garden represents
birds (or men) in harmony with God and the forces of Nature, whereas on this
hillside the huge "noyse" is "the harmony of created Nature, . . . not a
favorable omen for the proceedings about to take place."[36] The speech of the
royal tersel is couched in the language of courtly love:

> Unto my soverayn lady, and not my fere,
> I chese, and chese with wil, and herte, and thought,
> The formel on youre hond, so wel iwrought,
> Whos I am al, and evere wol hire serve,
> Do what hire lest, to do me lyve or sterve.
>   (416-420)

It is not necessary to give here his entire speech; five lines tell its
nature.

Like the De Planctu Naturae of Alanus de Insulis, which Chaucer
himself cites, this assembly develops the theme of opposition between Nature
and Venus, between the harmony of natural order in creation and the disorder
of man's perversion of that natural order. The tersel's speech itself
reverses the order of nature for that of the court. His proposal is to the
"soverayn lady, and not my fere." His attraction to the formel eagle
apparently stems from the fact that she sits on the hand of the goddess, not
from any virtue of her own. It is royal favor he is courting, not the lady
alone for herself.

When the uppoer ranks of birds cannot agree, the lower members must wait; but eventually they also fall to arguing among themselves in their thwarted efforts to solve the dilemma. Not until the formel eagle herself announces her decision to sacrifice her own love life for the "commune profit" and not to "serve Venus ne Cupide / Forsothe as yit" (652-653) can Nature put things back in order, allow the birds to make their own choices, and adjourn. Then, says Chaucer, harmony returns, "And, Lord, the blisse and joye that they make!" (669).

Like Scipio, Chaucer the dreamer has seen the disharmony that can result when men or birds too narrowly seek worldly fame. When royal tersels cannot agree because they all want the formel eagle who sits on the hand of the queen, and each must not be outdone by the other, the entire universe of Nature is thrown out of harmony. And when such disharmony takes place, it affects the worm eaters and the seed eaters as well. No part of Creation can be exempt. The "commune profyt" of all is threatened by the disregard and self-centeredness of even one. Harmony in creation is the concern of all, the responsibility of each.

In The House of Fame and The Parliament of Fowls, we have celestial ascents as dreams in which the poet-dreamer is taken by a guide to the place in which he learns about harmony in creation; the choice to be made between celestial and earthly, true and false love. In Troilus and Criseyde, the story is again one of love. But the ascent, rather than in the dream technique of Cicero or Dante, is more in the tradition of Plato or Lucan--the ascent of the soul after death in battle.

The ascent of Troilus has presented Chaucer scholars with several complex problems, most of which have seemed insoluble through the years: to what sphere did Troilus ascend? Why did Troilus laugh, or at what did he laugh? What degree of understanding may we ascribe to him in the end? These are the three, perhaps, that have been most persistent; and of course they are related. The cause and direction of Troilus' laughter hinges upon his acquired understanding, and both of them have a close relationship to his ascent into the spheres. Close to these problems is a fourth consideration of whether this ascent, and indeed the epilogue as a whole, is an integral part of the poem or a tacked-on moral that does not belong there. Such is the view of Walter Clyde Curry, who has called the entire epilogue "dramatically inappropriate" and who maintains that "this Troilus is in no sense to be identified with that Troilus who suffers for love, struggles against an inescapable destiny, and dies like a hero."[37] It appears that the questions of Troilus' laughter and his understanding should be considered in terms of his ascent itself, for it is the ascent of the soul and the perspective of spiritual perception that accompanies it that provide the basis for whatever change may be said to take place in Troilus' thinking.

Particularly perplexing to many scholars has been the problems of determining to which sphere Troilus ascended. Chaucer tells us,

> And when that he was slayn in this manere,
> His lighte goost ful blisfully is went
> Up to the holughnesse of the eighthe spere,
> In convers letyng everich element;
> And ther he saugh, with ful avysement,
> The erratik sterres, herkenyng armonye
> With sownes ful of hevenyssh melodie.
>   (Troilus and Criseyde, V. 1807-1813)

The problem arises from several difficulties. First, we need to know whether Chaucer was counting from the fixed stars inward or from earth outward. Cicero, in the Somnium Scipionis, counted inward:

> These are the nine circles, or rather spheres, by which the
> whole is joined. One of them, the outermost, is that of
> heaven; it contains all the rest, and is itself the supreme
> God, holding and embracing within itself all the other
> spheres; in it are fixed the eternal revolving courses of
> the stars. Beneath it are seven other spheres which revolve
> in the opposite direction to that of heaven. One of these
> globes is that light which on earth is called Saturn's. Next
> comes the star called Jupiter's. . . . and in the lowest
> sphere revolves the Moon, set on fire by the rays of the Sun.
> But below the Moon there is nothing except what is mortal and
> doomed to decay, save only the souls is given to the human
> race by the bounty of the gods, while above the Moon all things

are eternal. For the ninth and central sphere, which is the
earth, is immovable and the lowest of all. . . .38

It is, of course, important to recognize a crucial difference
between the point of view in the Somnium and in Troilus. Cicero is giving
us the explanation as Africanus tells it to Scipio, standing in the outermost
sphere, that of the Fixed Stars, and indicating the others as they lie beneath. On the other hand, Chaucer tells the story of Troilus from earth.
For him to begin at the point farthest from himself and count inward would
appear unreasonable. Boccaccio, on whom Chaucer based the ascent of Troilus
itself, names the spheres from the moon outward in the Teseide, not naming
earth but only the spheres that move. If Chaucer counted inward, following
Cicero, Troilus may be said to have ascended only to the moon; but if Chaucer
followed Boccaccio in this as he did in other aspects of the Teseide tale,
Troilus ascended to the fixed stars.

Plutarch, who followed Plato closely in his cosmology, tells us in
"The Face on the Moon," a segment of the Moralia, that the moon "measures off
the earth's shadow with few of her own magnitudes not because it is small but
she more ardently hastens her motion in order that she may quickly pass
through the gloomy place bearing away [the souls] of the good which cry out
and urge her on because when they are in the shadow they no longer catch the
sound of the harmony of heaven."39 It is, therefore, not impossible for the
spirit to hear the harmony when in the sphere of the moon. However, Chaucer
distinctly states that Troilus' ghost rose "up to the holughnesse of the
eighthe sphere, / In convers letyng everich element" (V. 1809-1810). Skeat
explains that the hollowness of the eighth sphere can refer only to the sphere
of the fixed stars, where "by taking up a position on the inner or concave
surface of this sphere, he would see all the planetary spheres revolving
within it."40 "Holownesse," Skeat has said just before, translates
Boccaccio's word concavita.41 He goes on to explain line 1810, "in convers
letyng, leaving behind, on the other side. When, for example, he approached
the sphere of Mars, it was concave to him; after passing beyond it, it

appeared <u>convex</u>. Some modern editions of the <u>Teseide</u> read <u>connessi</u>
(connected parts), but the right reading is convessi (convex surfaces), for
which Chaucer substitutes <u>convers</u>."[42] <u>Convessi</u> is the reading employed by
Robert K. Root, who cites Boccaccio's passage from <u>Teseide</u> in his notes to
Chaucer's lines. Chaucer has almost literally translated line by line from
Boccaccio in these three stanzas:

> Finito Arcita colei nominando,
> La quai nei mondo piu che altro amava,
> L'anima lieve se ne gi volando
> Ver la concavita del cielo ottava;
> Degli elementi i convessi lasciando,
> Quivi le stelle erratiche ammirava,
> L'ordine loro e la somma bellezza,
> Suoni ascoltando plen d'ogni dolcezza.
>
> Quindi si volse in giu a rimirare
> Le cose abbandonate, e vide il poco
> Globo terreno, a cui d'intorno il mare
> Girava e l'aere, e di sopra il foco,
> Ed Ogni cosa de nulla stimare
> A rispetto del ciel; ma poi al loco
> La dove aveva il suo corpo iasciato
> Gli occhi fermo aiquanto rivoltato.
>
> E Seco rise de'pianti dolenti
> Della turba lernea; la vanitate
> Forte dannando delle umane genti,
> Li qua' da tenebrosa cechitate,
> Mattamente oscurata nelle menti,
> Seguon del mondo la falsa biltate,
> Lasciando il cielo; e quindi se ne gio
> Nei loco a cui Mercurio la sortio.   43

Root makes the point that "Troilus, though able to see the planets
"with ful avysement," is near enough to Earth to distinguish the spot "ther
he was slayn."[44] However, Chaucer does not say that Troilus did distinguish
that spot in its detail but says simply that "at the laste, / Ther he was
slayn, his lokying down he caste" (1819-1820). Chaucer tells us that Troilus
left behind him all the elements, a statement repeated from Boccaccio's "degli

elementi i convessi lascianto." We know, of course, that under the Pythagorean and Platonic systems of cosmogony, the four elements are arranged in
layers—earth, water, air, fire—the lightest on top. Macrobius tells us of
the theory of a group of late Pythagoreans who "preferred to divide the universe into three successions of the four elements: in the first rank were
arranged earth, water, air, and fire, the last being a purer form of air
touching upon the moon."[45] In the second of the three successions, the order
was reversed and the elements more refined. Here, Moon contained the element
"earth" (and in some places we find the moon referred to as an ethereal earth),
Mercury and Venus contained water and air, and fire was in the Sun. In the
third rank, the order was reversed again and still more refined; and here the
element "earth" was in the Fixed Stars. It is of interest, then, to realize
that whether the eighth sphere is the Moon or the Fixed Stars, with this plan
both of those represent the element of earth, but in different degrees of
refinement; and in each instance the element of fire from one succession
impinges upon that of earth in the next.

   This succession of elements becomes still more important with
respect to Root's statement that "Dante and Beatrice mount upwards from the
summit of the Mount of Purgatory, through the heaven of fire, to the sphere of
the Moon. While passing through the heaven of fire, they first hear the
harmony of the spheres (Par[adiso] I. 77-81), as Troilus hears it from his
station in the 'eighte spere'."[46] However, in Canto II, Dante calls the Moon
"la prima stella"; and the fire through which he ascends coincides in time
with the harmony of the spheres. *"La novita del suono e 'l grande lume"*
(Paradiso I. 82).[47] It is the newness of the sound and the great light
together, he says, that inflame his heart with desire for greater knowledge.
This fire, then, is of the purer rank than the earthly. John D. Sinclair,
in his edition of Paradiso, comments, "at the opening of the narrative we find
Dante standing with Beatrice on the summit of Purgatory, 'pure and ready to
ascend to the stars' and looking at the sun. There he sees the glory of
things as unfallen man could bear to see it; but it is only when he looks

again at Beatrice while she is gazing above--the strong word _fissare_ is used four times for that intense absorption--that he is suddenly aware of the music of the spheres and of a 'great light' and comes, without his knowledge, nearer to the sun, brought into a new contact with heavenly realities."[48] Doubtlessly, all of these sources played an important part in Chaucer's thinking; and perhaps it is not unsupportable to surmise that he said "eighthe spere" and forbore to name either the Moon or the Sphere of the Fixed Stars in order to draw upon all of the sources available to him, not being limited by one of them but assimilating the significancies of all and thus enhancing his own. It has been apparent before this, particularly in The House of Fame in which Chaucer the dreamer and his eagle disagreed over the importance of his learning about the stars, that for Chaucer the significance of the astronomical concepts lay in their philosophical implications far more than in any scientific theories or knowledge for its own sake.

C. S. Lewis, in The Discarded Image, compares the ascents into the spheres of the souls of Chaucer's Troilus, Lucan's Pompey, and Boccaccio's Arcita of the Teseide (XI. 1 sq.). "Like Scipio," says Lewis, "he i.e., the ghost of Arcita observes how very small the earth is; like Pompey, he laughs; but not because his funeral, like Pompey's, is a hole-and-corner affair; it is the mourning he laughs at." Chaucer, he says, ignored this passage in writing of Arcita in the Knight's Tale but transferred it to Troilus. And Lewis amplifies upon his earlier (1936) statement to say, "Some have taken the laughter of Troilus to be embittered and ironic. I never thought so, and the descent of the passage, . . . seems to me to make it even less probable. I think all three ghosts--Pompey's, Arcita's, and Troilus'--laughed for the same reason, laughed at the littleness of all those things that had seemed so important before they died; as we laugh, on waking, at the trifles or absurdities that loomed so large in our dreams."[49]

Lucan, in the Pharsalia, tells of the ascent of the ghost of Pompey from the funeral pyre. "Soaring up from the burning-place," he relates, "it left the charred limbs and unworthy pyre behind, and sought the dome of the Thunderer."[50] This is the realm, of course, that Ovid describes as the "<u>Palatia Caeli</u>," the palace of Heaven, [51] along which dwell the en-nobled deities and which is called the Milky Way. Here, says Lucan, where our atmosphere and the spheres meet (see discussion of the pillar of the universe in Chapter 1), is the abode of heroes, "whose fiery quality has fitted them, after guiltless lives, to endure the lower limit of ether, and has brought their souls from all parts of the eternal spheres."[52]

We notice the two qualifications mentioned here--the dominance of fire as the highest of the four elements in the hero's character and his freedom from guilt. Lucan then stipulates a further condition: "to those who are coffined in gold and buried with incense that realm is barred." We are told that Pompey, killed in battle, mutilated by his enemies, and burned on the pyre, "had steeped himself in the true light of that region, and gazed at the planets and the fixed stars of heaven," and now he was able to under-stand; "he saw the thick darkness that veils our day, and smiled at the mockery done to his headless body."[53] At this point we see the smile that we hear reflected later in Troilus' laugh. Pompey looks down, filled with *se lumine vero*, at his own funeral, and sees it as a mockery. Says C. S. Lewis, "they made him laugh."[54]

Troilus, too, looks upon those who weep for him. His laugh is not mockery but that of a detached view. Like Scipio, his celestial ascent has enabled him to achieve perspective; he can now see things as a whole as he could not before. Here he is--free of all the despair and sorrow and fits of worry and frustration through which his blind desier for Criseyde has put him. He is free of all the fretting over what Fortune has been doing with him. He is free of all the banalities that those on earth must still endure. He has heard the music of the speres, and soon Mercury will direct him to whatever place is to be his abode; and he feels release and objectivity. These things he understands as he could not on earth; and yet, there are those whom he left behind, down there weeping for him. He laughs.

And down from thennes faste he gan avyse

> This litel spot of erthe, that with the se
> Embraced is, and fully gan despise
> This wrecched world, and held al vanite
> To respect of the pleyn felicite
> That is in hevene above; and at the laste,
> Ther he was slayn, his lokyng down he caste.
> And in hymself he lough right at the wo
> Of hem that wepten for his deth so faste;
> And dampned al oure werk that followeth so
> The lynde lust, the which that may not laste,
> And sholden al oure herte on heven caste.
> And forth he wente, shortly for to telle,
> Ther as Mercurye sorted hym to dwelle.
>   (V. 1814-1827)

Howard R. Patch, in a 1929 study, suggests that Troilus has learned "a sense of proportion."[55] Earlier, in 1918, Patch had said in regard to the ascent of Troilus, "after finishing his revision of Boccaccio's story, Chaucer added a passage from another tale by the Italian poet, borrowing from the Teseide to describe the ascent of Troilus to heaven and thus giving us Troilus'·final realization of his own mistake. The youth sees that here on earth our deeds follow our "blinde lust" (pleasure) when we really ought to set our hearts on heaven; and the poet warns 'yonge fresshe folkes' to realize the emptiness of worldly frivolity and turn from it to God."[56] D. W. Robertson calls the laughter ironic, "a laughter which [Chaucer], and Troilus from his celestial vantage point, would bestow on all those who take a sentimental attitutde toward such love as that between Troilus and Criseyde."[57]

Critical opinions have continued to proliferate on this topic of Troilus' laughter, ranging from Tatlock's opinion that the ending is "sudden and arbitrary" and merely added on,[58] to Alfred David's comment that the poem and epilogue form a unified whole that affirms earthly love as good even though transitory, with the greater Christian love going on beyond.[59] Root tells us, "Troilus laughs. He has not laughed before in the whole course of the poem since the very beginning of the story, before his first sight of Criseyde, when, himself heart-free, he made merry over the woes of foolish lovers. . . . He has taken life too seriously; now, like the poet who created him, he sees in life a high but comic irony."[60] Hamlet, comments Root, "dies with the unforgettably tragic words: 'the rest is silence.' The last we hear from Troilus is a peal of celestial laughter." Chaucer, he believes, has not handled the tale with sufficient seriousness for tragedy.[61]

Edmund Reiss, in his study of "Troilus and the Failure of Under-standing," makes the rather puzzling comment that Troilus only hears the music of the spheres but does not participate in it. It is difficult to understand how one could expect Troilus to participate in a music that is not produced by instrument or by voice, since, as Boethius explains and Chaucer knew, musica mundana, the harmony that exists in the universe, musica humana, the harmony within man, and musica instrumentis, produced music by voice or instrument, are not identical with each other. Only the last can be partici-pated in by man. Like Scipio or Dante, man can only become filled with the music of the spheres; he can play no part in producing it. Reiss also main-tains that Troilus has learned nothing, that he is bitter and scornful. He concludes that since, as Chaucer has said in the Tale of Melibeus, it is charitable to weep for the dead, Troilus in scorning his own mourners is committing what is, in the Parson's Tale, called "a wikked synne" (X [1] 635). From there, Reiss goes on to state that because, as he believes, Troilus' laughter is bitter and ironic rather than loving, his "final resting place is not in the spheres: he goes, rather, to that place 'ther as Mercurye sorted hym to dwelle' (1827)."[62] It may be, says Reiss, the ogdoad, "the sphere beyond the moving spheres where the souls of virtuous pagans tradition-ally went, or it may be Hades."[63] It seems important here to keep in mind that, although the action is placed in ancient Troy, Chaucer's Troilus is a Mediaeval knight in many respects. Chaucer calls him a knight in several instances, among them this passage from near the end of the poem:

In many cruel bataille, out of drede,
Of Troilus, this like noble knyght,
As men may in thise olde bokes rede,
Was seen his knyghthod and his grete myght.
(V. 1751-1754)

It may not be necessary, then, to doubt his ultimate salvation as many scholars have done. The whole concept of the celestial journey and harmony of the spheres has its basis, after all, in classical, pre-Christian litera- ture; and Troilus is in the tradition of other pagans such as Er, Pompey, and Scipio while at the same time he fits into the concept of Mediaeval chivalry and of Christians such as Dante. Troilus at last sees how small earth and earthly matters really are; and he laughs, I maintain, not bitterly, but with the release that comes with sudden illumination of the mind and perhaps astonishment at men on earth who still do not understand. D. W. Robertson says that Troilus laughs as he rises above the realm over which Fortune can rule. "When the flesh with its cumbersome desires has been left behind," he says, Troilus sees the foolishness of his earthly plight. There the 'jugement is more clear, the wil nat icorrumped.'"[64]

Troilus looks down after his ascent. So we recall, did Scipio; and Africanus cautioned him to look forward and not back. But perhaps, also Troilus shares the view of Dante, who also followed Scipio and who looked down as he was directed, in his case, to do.

> *Col viso ritornai per tutte quante*
> *Le sette spere, e vidi questo globo*
> *Tal, ch' lo sorrisi dei suo vil sembiante;*
> *E quel consiglio per migliore approbo*
> *Che l' ha per meno; e chi ad altro pensa*
> *Chiamar si puote veramente probo.*
> (Paradiso XXII. 133-138)

As he looks down through the seven spheres, he sees the pitifully small earth. Cary, in his very beautiful translation, renders these lines 136-138,

> It moved my smiles: and him in truth I hold
> For wisest, who esteems it least; whose thought
> Elsewhere are fix'd, him worthiest call and best.[65]

Dante, it will be observed here, smiles as did Pompey at his new insight. Troilus, a less inhibited and a younger man, laughs. To them, and to many another pilgrim of the spheres, the perspective is astounding—so much so that the viewer must look back again and again to see that it is so.

NOTES

[1] All quotations from Chaucer's works are from The Works of Geoffrey Chaucer, 2nd ed., ed., F. N. Robinson (Boston: Houghton Mifflin Company, 1957), hereafter cited as Works.

[2] Works, p. xxix.

[3] Macrobius, Commentary on the Dream of Scipio, trans. and ed., William Harris Stahl (New York: Columbia Univ. Press, 1952), pp. 87ff. References to this edition of Macrobius are hereafter cited as the Stahl edition.

[4] Macrobius, Stahl edition, p. 90.

[5] B. G. Koonce, Chaucer and the Tradition of Fame: Symbolism in The House of Fame (Princeton, New Jersey: Princeton Univ. Press, 1966), p. 58.

[6] Ibid., pp. 59-60.

[7] Ibid., pp. 181-188. Koonce's Biblical references are to the Douay Version, which of course is closest to the Mediaeval Vulgate. Thus, his citation on p. 182 to "the fourth book of Kings" is to 2 Kings 25 in the King James or later Protestant translations.

[8] Ibid., p. 65.

[9] Ibid., p. 66. Koonce gives a number of instances which imply a parallel with Christ's attributes of virtue in this respect.

[10] La Divina Commedia di Dante Alighieri, ed., C. H. Grandgent,

revised edition (Boston: D. C. Heath and Company, 1933). The passage seems
to perplex translators. The great nineteenth century clergyman-tranlator,
the Reverend Henry Francis Cary, renders line 118, "If it be lawful, Oh,
Almighty Power!" [The Vision; or Hell, Purgatory, and Paradise of Dante
Alighieri, trans., the Reverend Henry Francis Cary (New York: Worthington,
1844), p. 264]; and Dorothy L. Sayers, in a note, attributes the parallel
to the sounds of "Jove" and "Jehovah" [The Comedy of Dante Alighieri the
Florentine, Cantica II, Purgatory, trans., Dorothy L. Sayers (Baltimore:
Penguin Books, 1955), p. 116]. Much of this is peripheral to the present
study, but we may note that the name "Jupiter" is derived from Jovis-pater,
Jovis or Djovis meaning "the bright heaven," [The Oxford Companion to
Classical Literature, ed., Sir Paul Harvey (Oxford: Clarendon Press, 1937),
p. 232] which thereby seems to give Jupiter the appellation of a heavenly
father.

In succeeding references to the Divine Comedy, the three editions
named above are cited as the Grandgent edition, Cary edition, and Sayers
edition respectively.

[11]Koonce, p. 69.

[12]Charles S. Singleton, An Essay on the Vita Nuova (Cambridge,
Massachusetts: Harvard Univ. Press, 1949), pp. 74-75.

[13]Ibid., p. 91.

[14]For evidence of debate on this matter, as to whether the false
dawn is that of the moon or of the time shortly before sunrise (peripheral
here but of interest indirectly), see notes to the passage in the edition of
Grandgent and the translation of Cary and also the study by Francis
Fergusson, Dante's Drama of the Mind: A Modern Reading of the Purgatorio
(Princeton, New Jersey: Princeton Univ. Pres, 1953), p. 31.

[15]Kemp Malone, Chapters on Chaucer (Baltimore: Johns Hopkins Press,
1951), p. 54.

[16]The Bestiary: A Book of Beasts, Being a Translation from a Latin Bestiary of the Twelfth Century, T. H. White (New York: G. P. Putnam's Sons, 1960), pp. 105-107.

[17]Philip Schaff, A Dictionary of the Bible, 13th ed., (Philadelphia: American Sunday School Union, 1880).

[18]Ibid., p. 246.

[19]Chaucer and the Tradition of Fame, p. 81.

[20]Ibid., pp. 207ff.

[21]Edith Hamilton, Mythology (Boston: Little, Brown and Company, 1942), p. 40.

[22]J. A. W. Bennett, Chaucer's Book of Fame (Oxford: Clarendon Press, 1968), p. 178.

[23]Koonce, p. 252. Koonce cites a number of references, including Apocalypse 18 (Revelation 18) in which the angel of great authority appears, and Ezekiel 19: 8-9 in which a cage is employed as an image of the captivity of the Hebrews.

[24]Bennett, Chaucer's Book of Fame, p. 178.

[25]Ambrosii Theodosil Macrobil, Commentarii in Somnivm Scipionis, ed., Iacobus Willis (Leipzig, Germany: G. B. Teubner Verlagsgesellschaft, 1970).

[26]Macrobius: Commentary on the Dream of Scipio, trans. and with an Introduction and Notes, William Harris Stahl (New York: Columbia Univ. Press, 1952), p. 52. The probable extent of Chaucer's knowledge of the Commentary is discussed by Stahl on pp. 52-55.

[27]Bernard F. Huppe and D. W. Robertson, Jr., Fruyt and Chaf: Studies in Chaucer's Allegories (Princeton Univ. Press, 1963), p. iii.

[28]J. A. W. Bennett, The Parlement of Foules: An Interpretation

(Oxford: Clarendon Press, 1957), p. 63.

[29]Works, p. 794.

[30]Cicero, De Re Publica, De Legibus, trans., Clinton Walker Keyes (Cambridge, Massachusetts: Harvard Univ. Press [Loeb Library], 1951), VI. 12. p. 265. Unless otherwise noted, all quotations from the Somnium Scipionis, De Re Publica Book VI, are from this edition, hereafter cited as the Loeb edition. I have not, however, always followed Keyes' translation. Where I have done so, it is so indicated. I have done so in the quotation to which this note is attached.

[31]Cicero, De Re Publica, etc., Loeb edition, VI. xix, p. 272.

[32]Ibid., VI. xiii, p. 264.

[33]D. P. Simpson, Cassell's New Latin Dictionary (New York: Funk and Wagnall's, 1959), entry (3) under 2 caelum.

[34]Loeb edition, VI. xxiv-xxvi, passim, pp. 278-282. Cicero says much the same also in Tusculan Disputations, I. 53-55. The idea in Plato's Phaedrus 245C-E.

[35]Fruyt and Chaf, p. 118.

[36]Ibid., p. 124.

[37]Walter Clyde Curry, Chaucer and the Medieval Sciences (New York: Barnes and Noble, revised edition, 1960), p. 297.

[38]Cicero, De Re Publica, etc., Loeb edition, VI. xvii, pp. 268-271.

[39]Plutarch, Moralia XII, trans. and ed., Benedict Einarson and Phillip H. DeLacy (Cambridge, Massachusetts: Harvard Univ. Press [Loeb Library], 1967), pp. 207-209.

[40]The Complete Works of Geoffrey Chaucer, ed., W. W. Skeat (Oxford: Clarendon Press, 1894-97), Volume 2, pp. 504-505.

[41]Ibid., p. 504.

[42] Skeat, p. 505.

[43] The Book of Troilus and Criseyde by Geoffrey Chaucer, ed., Robert K. Root (Princeton, New Jersey: Princeton Univ. Press, 1926, 1954), p. 560.

[44] Ibid., p. 561.

[45] Stahl edition, p. 132.

[46] Root, p. 561.

[47] Grandgent edition, p. 659.

[48] Dante Alighieri, The Divine Comedy, Vol. III, Paradiso, trans. and ed., John D. Sinclair (New York: Oxford University Press Galaxy , 1961), pp. 28-29.

[49] C. S. Lewis, The Discarded Image (Oxford: Oxford Univ. Press, 1958), p. 34.

[50] Lucan, The Civil War [Parsalia], trans., J. D. Duff (New York: G. P. Putnam's Sons [Loeb Library], 1928), IX, pp. 504-505.

[51] Ovid, Metamorphoses, trans., Frank Justus Miller (Cambridge, Massachusetts: Harvard Univ. Press [Loeb Library], 1950), I, p. 14.

[52] Lucan, p. 505.

[53] Ibid., p. 505.

[54] The Discarded Image, p. 33.

[55] Howard R. Patch, "Troilus on Determinism," Speculum, VI (1929), 225-243. Reprinted in Chaucer Criticism, Volume II, ed., Richard J. Schoeck and Jerome Taylor (Notre Dame, Indiana: University of Notre Dame Press, 1961), 71-85; p. 81.

[56] Howard R. Patch, "Troilus on Predestination," JEGP, XVII (1918), 399-423. Reprinted in Chaucer: Modern Essays in Criticism, ed., Edward Wagenknecht (Oxford: Oxford Univ. Press, 1959), 366-384; pp. 373-374.

[57]D. W. Robertson, Jr., "Chaucerian Tragedy," ELH, XIX (1952), 1-37. Reprinted in Schoeck and Taylor, II, 86-121; p. 117.

[58]J. S. P. Tatlock, "The Epilog of Chaucer's Troilus," Modern Philology, XVIII (1921), 625-629; p. 636.

[59]Alfred David, "The Hero of the Troilus," Speculum, XXXVII (1962), p. 570.

[60]Root, p. xlix.

[61]Ibid., p. 1.

[62]Edmund Reiss, "Troilus and the Failure of Understanding," MLQ, XXIX:2 (June, 1968), 131-144; p. 141.

[63]Ibid., p. 141.

[64]Robertson, p. 117.

[65]Cary edition, p. 544.

CHAPTER IV

THE ELIZABETHAN CONCORD OF WELL-TUNED SONGS

> If the true concord of well-tuned sounds,
> By unions married, do offend thine ear,
> They do but sweetly chide thee, who confounds
> In singleness the parts that thou shouldst bear.
> Mark how one string, sweet husband to another,
> Strikes each in each by mutual ordering,
> Resembling sire and child and happy mother,
> Who, all in one, one pleasing note do sing.
> (William Shakespeare,
> Sonnet 8, lines 5-12)[1]

If it is possible to separate the various aspects of the concept of the Harmony of the Spheres and say that any one of them predominates, for the Elizabethan world that one would be the idea of Concord, of mutual ordering. The harmony of music, of "humors," and of society share this common ground. Shakespeare, like his contemporaries, expresses the idea in terms of music within and between human beings. This is the human music, the concord that exists within man as a microcosm; and, says the poet, it can be expressed truly only when there is harmony among human beings, between man and woman as husband and wife, between parents and children, between those who love.

Boethius divided music into three main types. For the English Renaissance with its synthesis of classical and Christian backgrounds and various contributions to the network of ideas, four main classifications may be discerned: _divine music_, the archetype in Platonic terms of which all others are imitations; _created music_, dependent upon the divine music and expressing the order and proportions of the created universe and each

75

individual form within that universe; _mundane music_, the harmony of the
creatures, the elements, and the natural forces of the world; and _human_
music, the concord within man as a microcosm, the harmony of "humors" by
which a man is kept a well-tuned instrument.[2] Of these, divine music is of
course beyond the capability of man even to imagine. Created music is the
Pythagorean Harmony of the Spheres.

Added to these four abstract classes of music is the fifth one--
musica practica--the equivalent of Boethius' _musica instrumentis_, by which
the others may be illustrated. We find mundane music and human music employed frequently by Elizabethan writers as expressions of the measure of
man and the world: for,

> The man that hath no music in himself,
> Nor is not moved with concord of sweet sounds,
> Is fit for treasons, stratagems, and spoils.
> The motions of his spirit are dull as night,
> And his affections dark as Erebus.
> Let no such man be trusted. Mark the music.
> (Merchant of Venice, V. i. 83-88)

Julius Caesar distrusts the lean and hungry Cassius who "hears no music"
(Julius Caesar, I. ii. 204); and Iago, in his malicious ambition to wreck
Othello, comments, "Oh, you are well tuned now, / But I'll set down the pegs
that make this music" (Othello, II. i. 201-202). It is the discord that
results when Othello and Desdemona cannot resolve the tones of each other's
hearts that is the prime tragedy of their tale. When, in Act III, scene iv,
for example, there is the issue of the lost handkerchief, both Othello and
Desdemona become so caught up in a type of hysteria that neither is able to
be frank and open with the other. Neither is capable of a clear thought,
of rational explanation. Othello's mind is obsessed by the discord of
suspicion, Desdemona's, of fear, to the extent that both fail to recall her
having offered him the handkerchief to assuage a headache and his having
said it was too small (III. iii. 282-289). That this discord remains un-
resolved is the failure in harmony that leads to the ultimate tragedy. We

are told in a bawdy discourse between the clown and musician (III. i. 1-21)
that wind instruments—presumably especially the nasal-toned bagpipe—were
not Othello's favorites and certainly not related to the music of the
spheres:

> . . . And the General
> So likes your music that he desires
> You, for love's sake, to make no more noise with it.
> . . .
> If you have any music that may not be heard, to 't again.
> But, as they say, to hear music the General does not greatly care.
> (III. i. 10-18)

Apollo's harp and the pipes are frequently employed to contrast
music of harmony and of passion. Lawrence J. Ross[3] reminds us of the story
of Midas, that critic who preferred the music of Pan's pipe (sometimes
referred to as a bagpipe) to Apollo's harp and was given a pair of ass's
ear for his lack of taste (in their view, apparently, no more taste than he
showed in wishing for a golden touch), and of the pipe-playing satyr,
Marsyas, whose instrument was designed to arouse the passions. Plato considered wind-instrument playing to be for pleasure only (see Gorgias, 501).
There are numerous references to the lack of positive spiritual value of
wind instruments in some traditions. In others, man is, by means of his
breath, considered to be "the pipe of God." For the Romantics of the late
eighteenth and nineteenth centuries, the wind itself becomes a parallel for
the music of the spheres. But the chief representative of the wind is the
simple Aeolian harp set in a window where the breeze might sweep its strings;
it is, then, a union of string and wind instrument. For a recognizable segment of Renaissance literary symbolism, however, the stringed instrument
represents celestial harmony or "Concord" and the wind instrument,—"passion"
of course referring here to any powerful emotional response, including anger
or violence as well as romantic infatuation, ribaldry, or other riotous
behaviour.

The concepts of harmony in music, harmony in the universe, harmony

in man and among men are inseparable. The Elizabethans' geocentric world
was feeling the effects of new scientific thought and on its way to becoming
more and more heliocentric; but it was above all theocentric. In the 1614
poem, "Doomsday" of Sir William Alexander, Earl of Stirling, we find:

> The stately Heavens which glory doth array,
> Are mirrours of God's admirable might;
> There, whence forth spreads the night, forth springs the day,
> He fix'd the fountaines of this temporall light,
> Where stately stars enstall'd, some stand, some stray,
> All sparks of his great power (though small yet bright.)
> By what none utter can, no, not conceive,
> All of his greatnesse, shadowes may perceive.
>
> What glorious lights through christall lanternes glance,
> (As alwaies burning with their Maker's love)
> Spheares keepe one musicke, they one measure dance,
> Like influence below, like course above,
> And all by order led, not drawne by chance,
> With majestie (as still in triumph) move.
> And (liberall of their store) seeme shouting thus;
> 'Looke up all soules, and gaze on God through us.'
>
> This pond'rous masse (though oft deform'd) still faire,
> Great in our sight, yet then a starre more small,
> Is ballanc'd (as a mote) amid'st the ayre;
> None knowes what way, yet to no side doth fall,
> And yearely springs, growes ripe, fades, falles, rich, bare,
> Men's mother first, still mistresse, yet their thrall.
> It centers Heavens, Heavens compasse it, both be
> Bookes where God's pow'r the ignorant may see. [4]

Order is found to be as much a part of the harmony as music, and one's right-
ful place in that order of far greater importance than mere humility for its
own sake. As each tone has its own place, and each planet its own orbit, so
each man has his proper place on the chain that unites all creation. As
Stirling continues later in the same poem,

> The world in soules, God's image cleare may see,
> Though mirrours brus'd when faine, sparks dim'd far flowne,
> They in strict bounds, strict bonds, kept captive be,

Yet walke ore all this all, and know not known;
Yea soare to Heaven, as from their burden free,
And there see things which cannot well be showne.
None can conceive, all must admire his might,
Of whom each atome gives so great a light.

In Shakespeare's <u>Richard II</u> the deposed king arrives at his final prison, Pomfret Castle, and begins to realize the causes of his overthrow: that "thoughts tending to ambition, they do plot / Unlikely wonders. . . ." (V. v. 18-19). He hears discordant music and remarks,

. . . How sour sweet music is
When time is broke and no proportion kept!
So is it in the music of men's lives.
                    (V. v. 42-44)

Ulysses, in <u>Troilus and Cressida</u>, gives us what appears to be a key to all of Shakespeare's tragedies when he explains to Agamemnon why it is that "after seven years' siege yet Troy walls stand" (I. iii. 12). The Greek forces contain too many discordances, too many "hollow factions":

. . . Degree being vizarded,
The unworthiest shows as fairly in the mask.
The heavens themselves, the planets and this center,
Observe degree, priority, and place,
Insisture, course, proportion, season, form,
Office, and custom, in all line of order.
. . .
. . . But when the planets
In evil mixture to disorder wander,
What plagues and what portents, what mutiny,
What raging of the sea, shaking of earth,
Commotion in the winds, frights, changes, horrors,
Divert and crack, rend and deracinate,
The unity and married calm of states
Quite from their fixure! Oh, when degree is shaked,
Which is the ladder to all high designs,
The enterprise is sick! . . .
. . .
Take but degree away, untune that string,
And hark! what discord follows! . . .
. . .

And the rude son should strike his father dead.
. . .
Then everything includes itself in power,
Power into will, will into appetite,
And appetite, a universal wolf,
So doubly seconded with will and power,
Must make perforce a universal prey,
And last eat up himself. . . .

(I. iii. 83-124, passim.)

This passage resounds with the theme of Julius Caesar, Macbeth, King Lear, and more. The world is a cosmos--an ordered and harmonic system in which each element has its place and in which each physical feature is inseparable from its moral equivalent. In Cicero's De Re Publica, Book II, Scipio says the same thing using musical terms:

> For just as in the music of harps and flutes or in the voices
> of singers a certain harmony of the different tones must be
> perserved, the interruption or violation of which is intolerable
> to trained ears, and as this perfect agreement and harmony is
> produced by the proportionate blending of unlike tones, so also
> is a State made harmonious by agreement among dissimilar
> elements, brought about by a fair and reasonable blending
> together of the upper, middle, and lower classes, just as if
> they were musical tones. What the musicians call harmony in
> song is concord in a State, the strongest and best bond of
> permanent union in any commonwealth; and such concord can
> never be brought about without the aid of justice.[5]

Thus it is that Macbeth--out of harmony with the macrocosm, out of harmony within his own microcosm--must have his own way, must be told what he insists the three witches tell him,

Though you untie the winds and let them fight
Against the churches; though the yesty waves
Confound and swallow navigation up;
Though bladed corn be lodged and trees blown down;
Though castles topple on their warders' heads;
Though palaces and pyramids do slope
Their heads to their foundations; though the treasure
Of nature's germens tumble all together,
Even till destruction sickens--answer me
To what I ask you.

(Macbeth, IV. i. 52-61)

Ross, grieved for the fate of the family of Macduff and for Scotland, has--
not the music of the spheres that can be heard only in a spirit of harmony--
but words "That would be howled out in the desert air, / Where hearing should
not latch them" (IV. iii. 194-195). Such have been the crimes of Macbeth
that have swept the land that they

> Strike Heaven on the face, that it resounds
> As if it felt with Scotland and yelled out
> Like syllable of dolor.
>   (IV. iii. 6-8)

This, then, is Discord. This is the same thing that is told us again two
centuries later by Ralph Waldo Emerson: "The reason why the world lacks unity,
and lies broken and in heaps, is because man is disunited with himself."[6]

Disharmony is the tragedy of King Lear as well, when, like what he
took to be Cordelia's ungratefulness, it has "wrench [his] frame of nature /
From the fixed place" (I. iv. 290-291). Holland has said that

> Shakespeare's imagination in King Lear seems more sublime,
> more poetic, more cosmic, somehow bigger than any stage can
> hold. . . . It does not have the perplexing enigmas of
> character that Hamlet did; what we find instead is a far more
> vast, more universal poetry, a poetry that asks over and over
> again, What is man's place in the universe? Does man stand
> at the center, ranked around and above him the angels and the
> animals and the planets, all, in a sense, pivoting upon him,
> on what happens on 'this great stage'? Or is man simply
> another animal among animals, squatting on a tiny ball of dirt
> spinning around an aged sun, one of a billion such suns, one of
> a billion such balls of dust spinning in an endless, purposeless
> galaxy in a vast and indifferent universe?[7]

Nature creaks and is split asunder in the universe of King Lear. Goneril
and Regan are "unnatural hags" (II. iv. 273), "disnatured" (I. iv. 274).
Edmund scoffs at his father's view of what is natural (I. ii. 1-15) and
strikes at his father's life. with all due caution not to read too much
into Shakespeare's art as a dramatist, but keeping in mind his function as
a dramatist to hold the mirror up to life, one asks how much this may have

had to do with reflecting the change in Elizabethan man's view of his universe. The story of Lear is an old one; but not until Shakespeare's version did the old king go mad and fight the storm, or Cordelia die in such a heartbreaking manner. King Lear was first performed at Christmas time, 1606. There are evidences that Shakespeare wrote it near the beginning of that year; the eclipses of the fall of 1605, for example, are mentioned. Galileo's impact had not yet been felt but soon would be. Copernicus' thought and studies were not unknown--though how well known is questionable-- and were the subject of debate. Elizabethans still thought of their universe as man and earth centered, but gradually they could feel it slipping away from them. How much of this is in Lear?

There were other factors to disturb the complacency of Elizabethan harmony. This was the age of exploration--strange people in strange lands followed other customs. How dependable, how unshakeable, was their world? As G. Wilson Knight points out, "the thought of 'nature' is as ubiquitous here as that of 'death' in Hamlet, 'fear' in Macbeth, or 'time' in Troilus and Cressida."[8]

E. M. W. Tillyard proposes that "the conception of order . . . must have been common to all Elizabethans of even modest intelligence." A great number of discussions of cosmology and order were available at several intellectual levels. Tillyard points out, too, that

> the negative implication was even more frequent and emphatic.
> If the Elizabethans believed in an ideal order animating
> earthly order, they were terrified lest it should be upset,
> and appalled by the visible tokens of disorder that suggested
> its upsetting. They were obsessed by the fear of chaos and
> the fact of mutability; and the obsession was powerful in
> proportion as their faith in the cosmic order was strong.
> To us chaos means hardly more than confusion on a large scale;
> to an Elizabethan it meant the cosmic anarchy before creation
> and the wholesale dissolution that would result if the pressure
> of Providence relaxed and allowed the law of nature to cease
> functioning. Othello's 'chaos to come again' or Ulysses's
> 'this chaos, when degree is suffocate,' cannot be fully felt
> apart from orthodox theology.[9]

On the other hand, there were hope and security in the ideas of the new astronomy of Copernicus. This does not mean that, the new astronomy supplanted the old quickly and easily. Many were reluctant to change, partly because they did not like the idea of losing the center position, partly because it did not seem possible to believe that earth—and they—were in motion, and no doubt partly simply because it is never easy to change. Tycho Brahe developed a sort of compromise in which the sun circled earth, and the other planets circled the sun. Thomas Digges, the English astronomer who died in 1595, wrote in his treatise, A Perfect Description of the Celestial Orbs,

Therefore need we not be ashamed to confess this whole globe of Elements enclosed with the Moon's sphere, together with the Earth as the Centre of the same, to be by this great Orb, together with the other Planets about the Sun, turned, making by his revolution our year. And whatsoever seems to us to proceed by the moving of the Sun, the same to proceed indeed by the revolution of the Earth, the Sun still remaining fixed & immovable in the middest. And the distance of the Earth from the Sun to be such, as being compared with the other Planets, maketh evident alterations and diversity of Aspects; but if it be referred to the Orb of stars fixed, then hath it no proportion sensible, but as a point or a Center to a circumference—which I hold far more reasonable to be granted, than to fall into such an infinite multitude of absurd imaginations, as they were feign to admit that will needs wilfully maintain the Earth's stability in the Centre of the world. But rather herein to direct ourselves by that wisdom we see in all God's natural works, where we may behold one thing rather endued with many virtues and effects, than any superfluous or unnecessary part admitted.

And all these things, although they seem hard, strange, & incredible, yet to any reasonable man that hath his understanding ripened with Mathematical demonstration, Copernicus in his Revolutions, according to his promise, hath made them more evident and clear than the Sunbeams. These grounds therefore admitted, which no man reasonably can impugn, that the greater orb requireth the longer time to run his Period: The orderly and most beautiful frame of the Heavens doth ensue.[10]

For Digges, it is above all else orderly for the sun to be in the center of
the universe, for "In so stately a temple as this, who would desire to set
his lamp in any other better or more convenient place than this, from whence
uniformly it might distribute light to all. For not unfitly it is of some
called the lamp or light of the world, of others the mind, of others the
Ruler of the world."[11] What, then, is reasonable and orderly is not to be
feared. Order is evidence that the Harmony of the Spheres is the true
concord, a reflection of the divine music and a model for the human. It is
when the harmony is broken that tragedy ensues.

If King Lear is a tragedy of storm, The Tempest is its contrary
image. This 1610 comedy was written at the close of the time of pan-psychical
occult sciences but before naturalistic science had achieved its dominating
influence on the thoughts of ordinary men. The occult that forms the basic
actions here is white magic--theurgy--as opposed to black magic. Theurgy,
as differentiated from geoty, comes to us from the fourth century De
Mysteriis of Iamblichus. Whether Shakespeare learned of it firsthand or
through conversations with Ben Jonson or another scholar is not clear, The
theurgist, in this case Prospero, is one who controls the activities of
nature by subjugating the guardian spirits to his will. Caliban, whose
name is an anagram for "cannibal," hence the savage man, and Ariel, creature
of air and fire, hence the finer and higher elements, present the two
extremes between which the alchemy must work.

The Tempest is full of music--"I' th' air or th' earth," played on
drum (tabor) and pipe by the invisible Ariel, "picture of Nobody." Music
pervades everything. "The isle is full of noises, / Sounds and sweet airs
that give delight and hurt not" (III. ii. 144-145). The accusation of Alonzo,
Sebastian, and Antonio by Ariel is accompanied by music. When, after the
usurpers have been punished, Ariel moves Prospero to forgiveness and pity,
and the old theurgist abjures his "rough magic," he calls upon, not Ariel's
pipe and tabor, but

```
    Some heavenly music . . .
    To work mine end upon their sense, that
    This airy charm is for . . .
                          (V. i. 52-54)
```

Now he will break his staff and bury his book--a move that tempts many scholars to call this Shakespeare's own farewell to the magic of the theater. As Hardin Craig has said, "having set all wrong things right, he will ascend still higher in the scale of spiritual being to the Platonic absolute, the all-embracing unity, in which mundane matters have no part, or rather are controlled without effort by supreme wisdom and supreme goodness."[12] The affairs of men can now be partially resolved with the assistance of "a solemn air, and the best comforter / To an unsettled fancy" (V. i. 58-59).

For Shakespeare, harmony is always of importance in the characterization of men. Cleopatra, who calls herself fire and air (but who is certainly no Ariel), says of dead Antony,

```
    His face was as the heavens, and therein stuck
    A sun and moon, which kept their course and lighted
    The little O, the earth.
    . . .
    His legs bestrid the ocean. His reared arm
    Crested the world. His voice was propertied
    As all the tuned spheres, and that to friends.
    But when he meant to quail and shake the orb,
    He was as rattling thunder. . . .
                      (Antony and Cleopatra, V. ii. 79-86)
```

There is the harmony between the elemental and spiritual in this same Antony's earlier tribute to the fallen Brutus, in whom the elements "so mixed in him that Nature might stand up / And say to all the world, 'This was a man.'" (Julius Caesar, V. v. 73-75). The tribute is well spoken to show the character of its speaker, of whom it was later to be said,

```
    . . . his delights
    Were dolphinlike, they showed his back above
    The element they lived in.
                      (Antony and Cleopatra, V. ii. 88-90)
```

though that eulogy is open to some doubt. Delights in the pleasures of this earth would not be those that would provide a way to the spheres, and Antony placed even the Roman Empire beneath his pleasure in Cleopatra.

In a great many of his plays, Shakespeare has combined the use of musica practica and the symbolic Harmony of the Spheres. Thus the one serves as the perceptible evidence of the other. In Henry VIII, instrumental and spherical music are combined when the suffering Katherine requests,

> . . . Good Griffith,
> Cause the musicians play me that sad note
> I named my knell, whilst I sit meditating
> On that celestial harmony I go to.
> (IV. ii. 77-80)

She sleeps, and in her vision is visited by garland-bearing beings

> . . . whose bright faces
> Cast thousand beams upon me, like the sun
> [And] promised me eternal happiness.
> (IV. ii. 88-90)

After this, instrumental music sounds harsh and heavy to her ears.

There is harmony in the well-tuned spheres, discord when the string is untuned, concord again when "the fingers of the powers above do tune / The harmony of the peace" (Cymbeline, V. v. 466-467). Shakespeare knows well how to finger the harp, blending its tones so that they "become the touches of sweet harmony."

If such tragedies as Othello, King Lear, and Macbeth provide accounts of the conditions and results of discord, the later plays, of which Pericles is of course the culmination, bear witness to the triumph of concord. Theodore Spencer has commented that in the tragedies we have the appearance of good but the reality of evil, whereas "in the later plays the appearance may be evil, but the reality is invariably good."[13] Shakespeare's vision now is one of the rebirth of human hope after apparent defeat, and it is miraculous and accompanied by the wonder that can best be expressed by celestial harmony. It is the music of the viol that brings Thaise out of her "death" to new life (Pericles, III. ii. 88-96); and Pericles, with the return of Marina, whom he had believed dead, hears the Music of the Spheres:

> I embrace you.
> Give me my robes. I am wild in my beholding.
> O Heavens bless my girl! But, hark, what music?
> Tell Helicanus, my Marina, tell him
> O'er, point by point, for yet he seems to doubt
> How sure you are my daughter. But what music?
>
> Helicanus: My lord, I hear none.
>
> Pericles: None!
> The music of the spheres! List, my Marina.
>
> Lysimachus: It is not good to cross him. Give him way.
>
> Per.: Rarest sounds! Do you not hear?
>
> Lys.: My lord, I hear.
>
> Per.: Most heavenly music!
> It nips me unto listening, and thick slumber
> Hangs upon mine eyes. Let me rest.
> (Pericles, V. i. 223-236)

Pericles, then, at the climax of his dramatic and allegorical pilgrimage of the soul, is visited in his dream vision (a Shakespearean rarity) by Diana. She directs him to her temple at Ephesus, where he is to tell the story of the death of his beloved queen, and Diana promises him happiness, "by my silver bow." He does; and father, mother, and daughter are at last reunited. This union of family takes us back to Sonnet 8, quoted at the head of this chapter--"sire and child and happy mother, / Who, all in one, one pleasing note do sing."

It may be noted here that only in Shakespeare is it the moon goddess Diana who appears to Pericles. In Gower's story, it is "the highë God;"[14] and in Laurence Twine's prose narrative an angel appears to Pericles in his sleep.[15] Neither Twine nor Gower includes the episode in which

Cerimon, having discovered the body of Thaïse floating on the sea in its
waterproof casket, calls for "the rough and woeful music that we have"
(III. ii. 88) to sound and bring her back to life: "The viol once more.
How thou stirr'st, thou block! / The music there! I pray you, give her air"
(90-91). John H. Long comments that, in contrast with his precursors,
"Shakespeare is reflecting, we may suppose, the Renaissance belief in the
animating power of music."[16]

Just as <u>Pericles</u> abounds in music and begins with a storm at sea,
<u>Twelfth Night</u> is also a story of tempest and music. In a synesthetic mode
of expression, Duke Orsino of Illyria opens the first act:

> If music be the food of love, play on.
> Give me excess of it, that, surfeiting,
> The appetite may sicken, and so die.
> That strain again! It had a dying fall.
> Oh, it came o'er my ears like the sweet sound
> That breathes upon a bank of violets,
> Stealing and giving odor! . . .
> (I. i. 1-7)

Viola mourns a brother lost in a tempest at sea, a brother last seen tied to
a mast to keep afloat like the mythological singer, Arion, who was saved by
a dolphin charmed by his song. Music and its powers have appeared twice
before the play is much more than fifty lines along. <u>Twelfth Night</u> has been
called a symphony with its themes, variations, separations, reunions. In
the beginning, when tempest and music are separate, the play is tragic. In
the end, with a song, it concludes as a comedy. <u>Twelfth Night</u> may be seen
in part, then, as a study in the importance of harmony in love and in life
in all its aspects. Olivia tells Cesario (Viola), when he pleads the love
of his master, that she would rather hear him solicit her love for himself
"than music from the spheres" (III. i. 121). The love for which he pleads
is not in harmony with Olivia's mind. To plead for himself, so far as
Olivia knows, would fit her own concepts of the page boy she thinks he is.

Orsino's opening speech has already been cited for its suggestions of the spirit if not the letter of this harmony. I propose a further suggestion: in Viola and Olivia, we have two young girls who are at first out of harmony with their world because of grief but who become "tuned" in the end; and we have one malevolent instrument, Malvolio, who, remaining discordant, can only exit. When we consider Shakespeare's propensity for an effective pun, these names may be seen as anagrams for that instrument of true harmony, the viol, one of them "mal."

Norman Holland has also perceived a parallel of identities in The Merchant of Venice.[17] It will be recalled that the turning spheres in Plato's myth of Er are assisted by the three Fates, daughters of Necessity on whose spindle the spheres are mounted. Plutarch compares with moon, sun, and earth these three who in the assignment of souls to bodies give them order (harmony), mind, and body. "Of the three Fates, too," Plutarch continues, "Atropos enthroned in the sun initiates generation, Clotho in motion on the moon mingles and binds together, and finally upon the earth Lachesis too puts her hand to the task, she who has the largest share in chance."[18]

In Greek mythology as well, Paris was given a choice among three women--Hera, Athena, and Aphrodite. Norman Holland points out that in Shakespeare's play we have three caskets that bear the key to Antonio's future, and three brides in the end--Portia, Nerissa, and Jessica, the syllabic metrical pattern of whose names matches Paris' three choices. And just as Malvolio is the one viol that cannot be tuned, so is Shylock the one who is unmoved by music. As Holland says, "Neither harmony nor legend has charms for him."[19] The entire play is based upon the concept of perfect harmony. D. A. Stauffer writes, "the balanced and triumphantly organized themes, counter-themes, and plots moved to a close; and the ideal of a harmoniously comprehensive virtue--reason reconciled with generosity, common sense with warm personal passion--finds its final perfect symbol in the moonlit and melodious garden of the lovers. Music can, for the time, change man's nature; Paradise may be taken in through the ear; and if he lacks responsiveness to the proportions that make music, man may not be saved."[20]

Lorenzo's discourse on music is perhaps one of the most famous of all on this topic (V. i. 54-88). Its origin, of course, is in Plato's Timaeus. Critics who have pointed to Shakespeare's "inaccuracies" in the description of the orbs and cherubim have based their opinion on The Republic. Aside from substituting cherubim for sirens, Shakespeare is essentially "correct." Most pertinent here, perhaps, is this portion:

> Whoso, then indulges in lusts or in contentions and devotes himself overmuch thereto must of necessity be filled with opinions that are wholly mortal, and altogether, so far as it is possible to ·become mortal, fall not short of this in even a small degree, inasmuch as he has made great his mortal part. But he who has seriously devoted himself to learning and to true thoughts, and has exercised these qualities above all his others, must necessarily and inevitably think thoughts that are immortal and divine, if so be that he lays hold on truth, and in so far as it is possible for human nature to partake of immortality, he must fall short thereof in no degree; and inasmuch as he is for ever tending his divine part and duly magnifying that daemon who dwells along with him, he must be supremely blessed. And the way of tendance of every part by every man is one--namely, to supply each with its own congenial food and motion; and for the divine part within us the congenial motions are the intellections and revolutions of the Universe.[21]

Lorenzo, sitting by his beloved Jessica on a moonlit bank, combines his love for her and his love for universal harmony, saying, of the music of the spheres,

> There's not the smallest orb which thou behold'st
> But in his motion like an angel sings,
> Still quiring to the young-eyed cherubims.
> Such harmony is in immortal souls,
> But whilst this muddy vesture of decay
> Doth grossly close it in, we cannot hear it.
> (V. i. 59-65)

The soul, in Platonic and later Neoplatonic theory, knows its true being only when it is not imprisoned in the body. Thus Scipio, in Cicero's Somnium Scipionis, as we have seen earlier, is told by Africanus that that which men call life is really the death of the soul. It is during the ecstasy of the mystical experience that the soul of man is capable of hearing the music of the spheres.

Spenser's Fowre Hymns (1596) appeared contemporaneously with The Merchant of Venice (1595 or 1596). The literary ancestry from Renaissance Petrarchan and related Platonic and Neoplatonic origins are therefore assumed to be common to both. For Spenser, there is a progression from earthly love to earthly beauty, to heavenly love, to heavenly beauty, through contemplation. From the Middle Ages on, love had been considered as evidence of a desire for beauty; and the progression throughout contemplative methodology had long been one from earthly images of the heavenly to the heavenly original--a truly Platonic heritage. Boethius comments in The Consolation of Philosophy that the "harmonious order of things is achieved by love which rules the earth and the seas, and commands the heavens. . . . O how happy the human race would be, if that love which rules the heavens ruled also your souls!"[22] Spenser, in the second hymn, "An Hymne in Honour of Beautie," tells us,

> For love is a celestiall harmonie
> Of likely harts composed of starres concent,
> Which joyne together in sweet sympathie,
> To worke ech others joy and true content,
> Which they have harbourd since their first descent
> Out of their heavenly bowres, where they did see
> And know ech other here belov'd to bee.
>   (197-202)[23]

The third hymn, "An Hymne of Heavenly Love," opens with this invocation:

> Love, lift me up upon thy golden wings,
> From this base world unto thy heavens hight,
> Where I may see those admirable things
> Which there thou workest by thy soveraine might,

> Farre above feeble reach of earthly sight,
> That I thereof an heavenly hymne may sing
> Unto the God of Love, high heavens king.
> (1-7)

It appears from this that in Lorenzo's discourse to Jessica on the parallels and symbolism of harmony in love as in music, and on earth as in the celestial realm, there is much of the theocentric contemplation that Spenser used in the Fowre Hymnes. Joseph B. Collins, in his treatment of Christian Mysticism in the Elizabethan Age, says of theocentric contemplation, "this type was highly adaptable for descriptions of the heavens, and it answered the familiar cry of the mystic: If God's handiwork is of such beauty, how much more beautiful must be the place and the Person wherein all this beauty has its source!"[24] Where there is harmony, there are beauty and the path to the way on high where the perfect harmony and beauty are to be found. Where there is disharmony, there is all that is evil and tragic.

Much of this concept of the true life of the soul comes into Renaissance philosophy and literature through such philosophers as Plotinus and St. Augustine, who interpreted and built upon Platonism. The view of the soul common to all these thinkers was that of an immortal entity deprived of its true being as long as it is confined to the body. While so confined it is likely to forget its immortal nature if it thinks on earthly subjects too intently; and if that happens, the soul forgets the vision of the upper world from which it came and looks downward, mistaking shadows and imitations in the material world for reality. Hence, in Shakespeare, we have many examples of confusion between disguises, disguises that disappear when harmony is restored. As in The Merchant of Venice where Portia adopts a male identity in order to reveal truth and establish justice, so the soul is helped through contemplation to remove itself from its earthly bondage in the body and to adopt the wings of vision in order to recall to itself the truth of its heavenly being. And as, once justice and truth have been restored, Portia may reassume her normal appearance, so the soul that has reestablished its divine nature and has remembered its origins may reassume its normal function in the body to guide that mortal life in the heavenly way. Since the soul is the true self of the man, the true vision on the part of the soul is the highest form of human self-knowledge. And it is when a man truly knows himself that he is in harmony both within himself and with the universe and thus with God. Mundane music and human music then coexist. Macbeth casts off his self-knowledge and commits himself to the tragedy of discord. He knows well that "who dares do more than becomes a man is none" (I. vii. 47), but his "false face must hide what the false heart doth know" (82), and he commits himself to the crime and the tragedy that must ensue.

The Elizabethan age has been referred to as a nest of singing birds, and certainly there is an abundance of poetry to be found. It would be utterly impossible to survey the entire range of ideas of harmony and the music of the spheres in this period because of the great number of examples if nothing else. Also, the concept itself permits so many variations on the single theme that these constantly proliferate. One example of this type of variation, and one that gave rise to a great number of developments itself, is the analogy between the motion of the universe and harmony of the spheres and the motion of the dance. The three Graces, the dance of the Hours, and the continuous rounds of the spheres themselves are all interlinked. As Sir John Davies, in his long poem, Orchestra, expressed it,

> 'Dancing, bright lady, then began to be
> When the first seeds whereof the world did spring,
> The fire air earth and water, did agree
> By Love's persuasion, nature's mighty king,
> To leave their first discorded combating
> And in a dance such measure to observe
> As all the world their motion should preserve.
> Since when they still are carried in a round,
> And changing come one in another's place;
> Yet do they neither mingle nor confound,
> But every one doth keep the bounded space
> Wherein the dance doth bid it turn or trace.

> This wondrous miracle did Love devise,
> For dancing is love's proper exercise.[25]

Davies here unites in one figure the harmony of the four elements and of the
spheres under one guiding law, that of Love. The entire poem centers about
a defense of dancing to Penelope, the "queen" of Ulysses. Penelope is not
quite ready to accept the idea that the "frantic jollity" Antinous proposes
she learn is the same thing as the cosmic dance he purports it to be, and
the efforts of Antinous to persuade her lead to some very interesting comparisons.

Davies at one point seems to anticipate Dryden's famous lines that
at the end of the world "music shall untune the sky" when he says,

> What if to you these sparks disordered seem,
> As if by chance they had been scattered there?
> The gods a solemn measure do it deem
> And see a just proportion everywhere,
> And know the points whence first their movings were,
> To which first points when all return again,
> The axletree of heaven shall break in twain.

This is closely related, of course, to Plato's concept of the great year.

Fortune herself is part of the harmony and not a counteracting
force:

> But why relate I every singular,
> Since all the world's great fortunes and affairs
> Forward and backward rapt and whirled are,
> According to the music of the spheres;
> And Chance herself her nimble feet upbears
> On a round slippery wheel, that rolleth aye,
> And turns all states with her impetuous sway?

For the Elizabethans, then, the entire network of concepts surrounding Concord offered variations with unity, many aspects of harmony
within and between men and between men and the universe as well as within
the universe itself, expressed as the music of the spheres or as a cosmic
dance, as the ascent of the soul in contemplation, and as the earthly

imitation of these in performed music and dance. But with all these possible variations of expression, Elizabethans in general could agree on the point expressed by Davies in Orchestra,

> The richest jewel in all the heavenly treasure
> That ever yet unto the earth was shown
> Is perfect concord, the only perfect pleasure
> That wretched earth-born men have ever known;
> For many hearts it doth compound in one,
> That whatso one doth will, or speak or do,
> With one consent they all agree thereto.

NOTES

[1] All quotations from the works of William Shakespeare are from the edition of G. B. Harrison (New York: Harcourt Brace, 1948), which follows the Globe text.

[2] Music in English Renaissance Drama, ed., John H. Long (Lexington: University of Kentucky Press, 1968), p. vi.

[3] Lawrence J. Ross, "Shakespeare's Dull Clown and Symbolic Music," Shakespeare Quarterly LXVI (Spring, 1966), pp. 109-128.

[4] Sir William Alexander, Earl of Stirling, Doomes-day; or The Great Day of the Lord's Judgement, "The First Houre," in The Works of the English Poets from Chaucer to Cowper, ed., Dr. Samuel Johnson with additional lives by Alexander Chalmers, 21 vols. Volume 5, Shakespeare, Davies, Donne, Hall, Stirling, Jonson, Corbet, Carew, Drummond (London: J. Johnson, 1810), p. 318.

[5] Cicero, De Re Publica, De Legibus, trans. and ed., Clinton Walker Keyes (Cambridge, Massachusetts: Harvard Univ. Press [Loeb Library], 1928, 1961), Republic II. xiii, pp. 180-182.

[6]Ralph Waldo Emerson, "Nature," The Complete Essays and Other Writings of Ralph Waldo Emerson, ed., Brooks Atkinson (New York: The Modern Library, 1940), p. 41.

[7]Norman Holland, The Shakespearean Imagination (New York: Macmillan Company, 1964), p. 233.

[8]G. Wilson Knight, The Wheel of Fire (London: Methuen, 1949, 4th ed.), p. 179.

[9]E. M. W. Tillyard, The Elizabethan World Picture (New York: Random House [Vintage Books]), p. 12.

[10]Thomas Digges, "In Support of Copernicus," The Portable Elizabethan Reader, ed., Hiram Haydn (New York: Viking Press, 1946), 106-125; pp. 113-114.

[11]Ibid., p. 115.

[12]Hardin Craig, An Interpretation of Shakespeare (Columbia, Missouri: Lucas Brothers, 1948), p. 350.

[13]Theodore Spencer, Shakespeare and the Nature of Man (New York: Macmillan Company, 1942), p. 186.

[14]John Gower, Confessio Amantis, VIII. 1789. The English Works of John Gower, ed., G. C. Macaulay (Oxford: Oxford Univ. Press for Early English Text Society, 1900 [1957], 2 volumes), vol. II.

[15]Laurence Twine, The Pattern of Painful Adventures (1607). With respect to both Gower's and Twine's versions, see Ernest Schanzer's notes in the Signet Classic edition of Pericles, Prince of Tyre (New York: New American Library, 1965), pp. xxii and xxix. The selection from Gower is given on pp. 160-168; Twine, pp. 169-180.

[16]John H. Long, Shakespeare's Use of Music: The Final Comedies (Gainesville: University of Florida Press, 1961), p. 42.

[17] Holland, p. 95.

[18] Plutarch, _Moralia_, 16 volumes, ed., F. H. Sandbach (Cambridge, Massachusetts: Harvard Univ. Press [Loeb Library], 1969), XII, p. 221.

[19] Holland, p. 97.

[20] Donald Alfred Stauffer, _Shakespeare's World of Images: The Development of his Moral Ideas_ (New York: Norton, 1949), p. 65.

[21] Plato, _Timaeus_ in _Plato with an English Translation_ VII, trans. and ed., Reverend R. G. Bury (New York: G. P. Putnam's Sons, 1929 [Loeb Library]), p. 247.

[22] Boethius, _The Consolation of Philosophy_, trans. and ed., Richard Green (Indianapolis: Bobbs-Merrill Company, Inc. [Library of Liberal Arts], 1962), p. 41.

[23] _The Complete Poetical Works of Spenser_, ed., R. E. Neil Dodge (Boston: Houghton Mifflin Company, 1908).

[24] Joseph B. Collins, _Christian Mysticism in the Elizabethan Age_, Baltimore: Johns Hopkins Press, 1940), p. 211.

[25] Sir John Davies, "Orchestra," in _Silver Poets of the Sixteenth Century_, ed. Gerald Bullett (New York: E. P. Dutton [Everyman's Library], 1947), pp. 320-342.

CHAPTER V

MILTON AND THE NINE INFOLDED SPHERES

> But else in deep of night, when drowsiness
> Hath lockt up mortal sense, then listen I
> To the celestial Sirens' harmony,
> That sit upon the nine infolded Spheres
> And sing to those that hold the vital shears
> And turn the Adamantine spindle round,
> On which the fate of gods and men is wound.
> Such sweet compulsion doth in music lie,
> To lull the daughters of Necessity,
> And keep unsteady Nature to her law,
> And the low world in measur'd motion draw
> After the heavenly tune, which none can hear
> Of human mold with gross unpurged ear.
> ("Arcades" 61-73)[1]

For Milton, accomplished musician as well as poet, the way on high "before the starry threshold of Jove's Court" (Comus I) provided a special type of opportunity for justifying the ways of God to men, for viewing "this dim spot, / Which men call Earth," (5-6) and for enabling the

> Sphere-born harmonious Sisters, Voice and Verse
> . . .
> . . . to our high-rais'd fantasy to present
> That undisturbed Song of pure concent.
> ("At a Solemn Music" 2, 5-6)

In Book VII of Paradise Lost Milton shows us the "broad and ample road, whose dust is Gold / and pavement Stars" (577-78) by which "the great Creator from his work return'd / Magnificent, his Six days' work, a World" (567-568). By way of this cosmic pillar God would

Visit oft the dwellings of just Men
Delighted, and with frequent intercourse
Thither will send his winged Messengers
On errands of supernal Grace.

(570-573)

One of these messengers is the sociable Raphael who educates Adam and Eve.

Many scholars who contend that the pre-Copernican geocentric astronomy induced men to feel that Earth and Man are central in importance and that all revolves about them in intent and primacy also carry that view of man's world to an implication of egocentricity or even of egotism. On Christmas Day, 1968, while Apollo VIII was circling the Moon on its historic flight, Archibald Macleish wrote for the New York Times News Service:

> The medieval notion of the earth put man at the center of everything. The nuclear notion of the earth put him nowhere--beyond the range of reason even--lost in absurdity and war. This latest notion [i.e., the view of earth from the depths of space, "whole and round and beautiful and small as even Dante . . . had never dreamed of seeing it"] may have other consequences. Formed as it was in the minds of heroic voyagers who were also men, it may remake our image of mankind. No longer that preposterous figure at the center, no longer that degraded and degrading victim off at the margins of reality and blind with blood, man may at last become himself.
>
> To see the earth as it truly is, small and blue and beautiful in that eternal silence where it floats, is to see ourselves as riders on the earth together, brothers on that bright loveliness in the eternal cold--brothers who know now they are truly brothers.[2]

In 1935, Marjorie Nicolson wrote that "the difference between 'old' and 'new' is said to be found in the difference between generations who felt their earth the center of the universe and generations who have learned that their earth is no such thing."[3] What was important for the seventeenth century, she maintained, was not so much which astronomical system was correct, but rather a new awareness of the immensity of the universe: "It is this which troubles and enthralls; the solid earth shrinks to minute proportions, as man surveys the new cosmos; it is a tiny ball, moving in indefinite space, and beyond it are other worlds with other suns, all parts of a cosmic scheme which defeats im.gination."[4] This was part of that which led Milton, among others, "to an awareness of the vastness and the minuteness of the nature of the universe and of man."[5]

Yet, is this view so different from that which led Er and Scipio to look down from the Milky Way to perceive the smallness of the earth in the vastness of the universe, or the ghost of Chaucer's Troilus to contemplate the temporary nature of his earthly concerns and laugh within himself in astonishment and recognition of his changed values? True, for the ancient the earth was centric; but it is difficult to equate this belief with any implication of egocentric philosophy. If the centricity of earth was essential to classical and mediaeval philosophy, it appears to have generated ideas more humble than proud, concerned more with duty and responsibility than with pride. Arthur O. Lovejoy expresses the view that "the centre of the world was not a position of honor; it was rather the place farthest removed from the Empyrean, the bottom of the creation, to which its dregs and baser elements sank. The actual centre, indeed, was Hell; in the spatial sense the medieval world was literally diabolocentric. And the whole sublunary region was, of course, incomparably inferior to the resplendent and incorruptible heavens above the moon."[6] Dante's Hell, of course, was an inverted cone with its apex at the center of the earth. Pride itself was not only one of the seven deadly sins but basic and causative to most, if not all, of the others in that geocentric world; and there is little evidence that the change to a heliocentric universe with earth one of several sun-orbiting planets wrought any great change in man's susceptibility to that vice.

The most important consideration in all of this matter has always been the concept of harmony--horizontally among all of the creatures and vertically between the created earth and Heaven. It is through this harmony that order is maintained in and among the various levels of life. Milton's contemporary, Robert Fludd, produced one of several graphic representations of the Harmony of the Spheres, making use of the familiar musical instrument of the day, the monochord, as a framework for its depiction. The monochord came to be seen as a vertical scheme of the harmony among all three levels—Heaven, the spheres, and earth.

The seventeenth-century astronomer, Johannes Kepler, continued and expanded upon earlier demonstrations of actual musical relationships among the spheres. By computing the theoretical musical intervals according to the angular velocities of the planets from the sun, he proposed the following proportions as demonstrations of world harmony of which the musical harmony is the expression:

APPARENT DIURNAL MOVEMENTS

Saturn at aphelion	1' 46"	a.
at perihelion	2' 15"	b.
Jupiter at aphelion	4' 30"	c.
at perigelion	5' 30"	d.
Mars at aphelion	26' 14"	e.
at perihelion	38' 1"	f.
Earth at aphelion	57' 3"	g.
at perihelion	61' 18"	h.
Venus at aphelion	94' 50"	i.
at perihelion	97' 37"	k.
Mercury at aphelion	164' 0"	l.
at perihelion	384' 0"	m.

Employing these diurnal movements of the planets in their orbits, which, Kepler points out, are apparent from the viewpoint at the sun, we then arrive at the harmonies between two planets:

DIVERGING		CONVERGING	
$\dfrac{a}{d} = \dfrac{1}{3}$		$\dfrac{b}{c} = \dfrac{1}{2}$	Saturn--Jupiter
$\dfrac{c}{f} = \dfrac{1}{8}$		$\dfrac{d}{e} = \dfrac{5}{24}$	Jupiter--Mars
$\dfrac{e}{h} = \dfrac{5}{12}$		$\dfrac{f}{g} = \dfrac{2}{3}$	Mars--Earth
$\dfrac{g}{k} = \dfrac{3}{5}$		$\dfrac{h}{i} = \dfrac{5}{8}$	Earth--Venus
$\dfrac{i}{m} = \dfrac{1}{4}$		$\dfrac{k}{l} = \dfrac{3}{5}$	Venus--Mercury

Kepler noted, moreover, that because of eccentricities of the orbits, there were variations in the derived ratios; and, consequently, he presumed from the ratios given in the first section of this chart (which has been separated into its three parts here for clarity of presentation, the note being held until the last part) that certain concordances were present between the extremes of the apparent movements of the single planets. By this means he arrived at the third section of his calculations, the harmonies between the movements of each planet itself--that is, the harmony within the movement of each planet between its aphelion and perihelion extremes of distance from the sun:

Saturn	1' 48" :	2' 15" =	4 : 5, a major third;
Jupiter	4' 35" :	5' 30" =	5 : 6, a minor third;
Mars	25' 21" :	38' 1" =	2 : 3, a fifth;
Earth	57' 28" :	61' 18" =	15 : 16, a semitone;
Venus	94' 50" :	98' 47" =	24 : 25, a diesis;[7]
Mercury	164' 0" :	394' 0" =	5 : 12, an octave and a minor third.[8]

Since, in the course of a revolution, the planets' velocity would change, this theoretical tone would run through the entire range of the interval between the extremes already shown. Venus' almost circular orbit Kepler showed as possessing a single note, whereas the much more elliptical course of Mercury produces a much wider progression. These theoretical harmonies are given in modern musical notation by Mr. Elliott Carter, Jr., as shown below:[9]

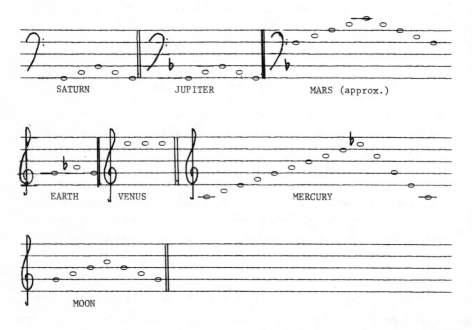

It goes beyond our needs in this study to attempt to delve into the complicated astronomical and mathematical calculations by which Kepler arrived arrived at the basis for his theories. These are to be found in most of his works passim, and they are particularly developed in the Epitome of Copernican Astronomy and in The Harmonies of the World. Much of his thinking depends upon an analogy between the geometry of the heavens and the geometry of five regular, solid shapes. This analogy is quite proper, says Kepler, "for the Creator, who is the very source of geometry and, as Plato wrote, 'practices eternal geometry,' does not stray from his own archetype. . . . It is consonant that if the Creator had any concern for the ratio of the spheres in general, He would also have had concern for the ratio that exists between the varying intervals of the single planets specifically and that the concern is the same in both cases and the one is bound in the other."[10]

What is important here for us is that the idea of an harmonious relationship within the universe was by no means a piece of pagan antiquarianism of which Milton had become enamored as a youth and had not cast off. Kepler's Harmonies first appeared in 1618 and 1619, the Epitome in 1620 and 1621. Milton's youthful "Second Prolusion" was composed probably in 1628 or 1629, nearly a decade later--a decade during which the new developments in the field of astronomy were having their profound effects upon the thinking of people in every part of the literate world. In the midst of the debate to which Milton refers in his essay, it was an accepted conclusion that if the music of the spheres was not certain it was at least probably and plausible. Kepler, as we have seen, in the midst of the Copernican revolution, still did not discard the music but related the harmony to the centric sun rather than the centric earth and considered it symbolically rather than realistically. The "Second Prolusion," delivered in the Public Schools with the title, "On the Music of the Spheres," is our earliest sure evidence of Milton's interest in astronomical matters. It is in its way as truly a companion for "On the Morning of Christ's Nativity" (1629) as De Doctrina Christiana is for Paradise Lost. How can Aristotle disparage the idea of the music of the spheres, asks Milton. Perhaps it is the very thing that soothes Atlas so that he does not drop his burden. With youthful urbanity and irony, Milton proceeds to show how useful such harmony would be. It is only because the insolent Prometheus by his theft of fire from Zeus brought sin and woe to man that we cannot hear this music. If our hearts were as pure as that of Pythagoras, surely we too could hear the song of the sirens as they ride upon the spheres. "Then we should be immune to pain, and we should enjoy the blessing of a peace that the gods themselves might envy" (p. 604). Compare this sentence with stanzas XIV and XV of the nativity ode:

XIV

For if such holy Song
Enwrap our fancy long,
    Time will run back, and fetch the age of gold,
And speckl'd vanity
Will sicken soon and die,
    And leprous sin will melt from earthly mold,
And Hell itself will pass away,
And leave her dolorous mansions to the peering day.

XV

Yea, Truth and Justice then
Will down return to men,
    Th'enamel'd <u>Arras</u> of the Rainbow wearing,
And Mercy set between,
Thron'd in Celestial sheen,
    With radiant feet the tissued clouds down steering,
And Heav'n as at some festival,
Will open wide the Gates of her high Palace Hall.

A few years earlier, it is true, the seventeen-year-old schoolboy, grieved at the deaths so close together of his idols, Lancelot Andrewes and Nicholas Fenton, had expressed the comfort of imagining himself "carried aloft, clear to the stars, like the venerable prophet of old, charioteer of a fiery chariot, who was caught up to heaven" (On the Death of the Bishop of Ely," pp. 24-25). The Latin elegy describes his feelings at being borne "through the ranks of the planets and the Milky Way" at an amazing speed but not terrified. "But here I fall silent," he concludes, "for who that is begotten of a mortal father can tell the delights of that place? For me it is enough to enjoy them forever" (II. 45-68 passim). Later, in the "Vacation

Exercise" of July, 1628, in which Milton hails his native language "that by
sinews weak / Didst move my first endeavoring tongue to speak," we find the
youth pleading for greater skill to express "some naked thoughts that rove
about / And loudly knock to have their passage out" (23-24). Yet he wishes
that his assigned topic were more worthy, something that might cause his
Muse to "search thy coffers round, / Before thou clothe my fancy in fit
sound:" and

> . . . passing through the Spheres of watchful fire,
> And misty Region of wide air next under,
> And hills of Snow and lofts of piled Thunder

might "sing of secret things (40-43, 45). In the same year, he wrote of his
dead infant niece as "above that high first-moving Sphere" ("On the Death of
a Fair Infant Dying of a Cough," 39).

These, however, are all prefatory to the great nativity ode that
marks Milton's coming of age both legally and as a poet. Professor Marjorie
Nicolson comments that although it "may still have been exercise and practice
to the young poet, . . . it is poetry in which if not full perfection, there
is greatness."[11] Herein all of the earlier thoughts concerning the harmonious
way on high are brought together. In this ode the Harmony of the Spheres is
consistently linked with the song of the angel host in a way that becomes
increasingly significant for an understanding of his thought. The shepherds
are spoken of as "chatting in a rustic row"

> When such music sweet
> Their hearts and ears did greet,
>   As never was by mortal finger struck
> ("On the Morning of Christ's
>   Nativity," IX, 93-95)

and Nature, hearing it,

> Now was almost won
> To think her part was done,
>   And that her reign had here its last fulfilling;

> She knew such harmony alone
> Could hold all Heav'n and Earth in happier union.
>   (X. 104-108)

Only then do we see "the helmed Cherubim / And sworded Seraphim" who are "Harping in loud and solemn choir." Milton tells us that such music "before was never made" since God set the constellations, hung the "well balanc't world," cast the deep foundations, and bid the waters "their oozy channel keep" (XII, passim). Now he addresses himself directly to the harmonious spheres in that beloved stanza:

> Ring out ye Crystal spheres,
> Once bless our human ears,
>   (If ye have power to touch our sense so)
> And let your silver chime
> Move in melodious time:
>   And let the Bass of Heav'n's deep Organ blow,
> And with your ninefold harmony
> Make up full consort to th'Angelic symphony.
>   (XIII, 125-132)

But what if we should hear the celestial harmony? We have already noted that eventuality--the release of man from sin and death, the return to the Golden Age of Eden. Truth and justice, then, "will down return to men, / Th'enameled Arras of the Rainbow wearing" (XV, 142-143), and thus combine the perfect ninefold musical harmony with the harmony of the colors. It cannot, however, yet be; for

> The Babe lies yet in smiling infancy,
> That on the bitter cross
> Must redeem our loss;
>   So both himself and us to glorify.
>   (XVI, 151-154)

Much must happen, much must be lost and won, before man can once more hear those beautiful harmonies.

Yet Milton was not to leave off se rching for answers to the puzzles of the universe, though man could not hear again the spheric melodies.

Who was "that first being--eternal, incorruptible, unique yet universal, coeval with the heavens and made in the image of God" who could hear the music? Was he "a comrade of the eternal stars who goes wandering through the ten-fold spheres of heaven or inhabits the neighbor of this world, the moon?" ("On the Platonic Idea as Understood by Aristotle," 9-12, 20-25); and what was it that he heard? Sometimes Milton thinks of it as joyful music "untwisting all the chains that tie / The hidden soul of harmony" ("L'Allegro," 143-144). Again, at a melancholy midnight hour, he writes of sitting all night to

> . . . unsphere
> The spirit of Plato to unfold
> What Worlds, or what vast Regions hold
> The immortal mind that hath forsook
> Her mansion in this fleshly nook.
> ("Il Penseroso," 88-92)

Pensively he asks,

> And as I wake, sweet music breathe
> Above, about, or underneath,
> Sent by some spirit to mortals good,
> Or th'unseen Genius of the Wood.
> (151-154)

In "Arcades," this Genius of the Wood tells of her duties in protecting the woods in the verses appearing at the head of this chapter.

Was man, then, utterly to be deprived of this glorious music because of his fall? The two "pledges of Heav'n's joy," those sisters, Voice and Verse, already mentioned ("At a Solemn Music," 1-6), offer promise of an image of heavenly music that could, through men's harmony on earth, bring them closest to the ultimate harmony, as it is called by Procius,[12]

> That we on Earth with undiscording voice
> May rightly answer that melodious noise;
> As once we did, till disproportion'd sin
> Jarr'd against nature's chime, and with harsh din
> Broke the fair music that all creatures made

> To their great Lord, whose love their motion sway'd
> In perfect Diapason, whilst they stood
> In first obedience and their state of good.
>
>   ("At a Solemn Music," 17-24)

Here, Milton has mingled the music of the spheres with an answering motif from the creatures in a perfect counterpoint of accord.

     Comus gives us a slightly different view of Milton's treatment of the harmony of the spheres because it is in a different genre from the other poems mentioned. In this rather atypical masque on the theme of Virtue's triumph over Vice, the "Attendant Spirit" tells us of the vantage point from which he views the actions of mortals:

> Before the starry threshold of Jove's Court
> My mansion is, where those immortal shapes
> Of bright aerial Spirits live inspher'd
> In Regions mild of calm and serene Air,
> Above the smoke and stir of this dim spot
> Which men call Earth, . . .
>
>   (1-6)

     The reference here is to Ovid's description, in Book I of the _Metamorphoses_, of the Milky Way as the path of ascent to the throne of Jove, along which are enthroned the noble deities. The passage has been discussed in Chapter I, but, for the sake of comparison with this quotation from _Comus_, we should look again at that portion that is pertinent, especially in the Latin:

> _Est via sublimis, caelo manifesta sereno;_
> _lactea nomen habet, candore notabilis ipso._
> _hac iter est superis ad magni tecta Tonantis_
> _regalemque domum: dextra laevaque deorum_
> _atria nobilium valvis celebrantur apertis._
> _plebs habitat diversa locis: hac parte potentes_
> _caelicolae clarique suos posuere penates;_
> _hic locus est, quem, si verbis audacia detur,_
> _haud timeam magni dixisse Palatia caeli._[13]
>
>   (168-176)

This *via sublimis*, this sublime way on high, Ovid tells us, is manifest in a serene sky--Milton's "regions mild of calm and serene Air." A little further on in Comus, Milton mentions the crown given by Virtue "after this mortal change, to her true Servants / Amongst the enthron'd gods on Sainted seats" (10-11). Here, then, rather than an Er, Scipio, Pompey, or Troilus ascending the Milky Way to look back upon his fellow mortals and wonder at the spot called Earth, we have a spirit who abides along that way, the threshold of Jove's court, and surveys and occasionally descends to intervene with mortals in their daily lives, their temptations and dangers, as well as their triumphs. He is not a member of the court of deities, but his abode is con-tiguous to it; he does not rule mortals but may assist them.

Just as the Attendant Spirit is more fairy-like and more magical than heavenly, but dwells along a heavenly way, so Comus, son of Circe, the counter-type of those spirits of the spheres, with "midnight shout and revelry" has his abode with "pert Fairies and the dapper Elves" of the lower air--i.e., the region between Earth and the Moon. He proposes with apparent irony that

> We that are of purer fire
> Imitate the Starry Choir,
> Who in their nightly watchful Spheres,
> Lead in swift round the Months and Years.
> (111-114)

We can compare this with the daytime scene in Book V of Paradise Lost in which Raphael, who also has descended from above to intercede in the ways of man, describes the presentation by God of His Son to the angels:

> That day, as other solemn days, they spent
> In song and dance about the sacred Hill,
> Mystical dance, which yonder starry Sphere
> Of Planets and of fixt in all her Wheels
> Resembles nearest, mazes intricate,
> Eccentric, intervolv'd, yet regular
> Then most, when most irregular they seem:
> And in thir motions harmony Divine

> So smooths her charming tones, that God's own ear
> Listens delighted.
>
> (V. 618-627)

Here is the court, not of Jove, but of God, where angels rather than mere
"aerial Spirits" live amid the harmony. Earlier in Book V., Eve's dreams
have been invaded by the toady Satan who, like Comus, presents a night-time
parody of the pure harmony of Heaven--a parody in which the celestial
pleasures take on a baseness that is an imitation of those joys:

> Why sleep'st thou Eve? now is the pleasant time,
> The cool, the silent, save where silence yields
> To the night-warbling Bird, that now awake
> Tunes sweetest his love-labor'd song; now reigns
> Full Orb'd the Moon, and with more pleasing light
> Shadowy sets off the face of things; in vain,
> If none regard; Heav'n wakes with all his eyes,
> Whom to behold but thee, Nature's desire,
> In whose sight all things joy, with ravishment
> Attracted by thy beauty still to gaze.
>
> (V. 38-47)

The harmony of creation is perfectly perverted here by Satan, who makes even
the innocent nightingale sound like a courtly lover, and Eve is tempted to
idolize her own beauty. A little later, Satan tempts Eve still further to

> Taste this, and be henceforth among the Gods
> Thyself a Goddess, not to Earth confin'd,
> But sometimes in the Air, as wee, sometimes
> Ascend to Heav'n, by merit thine, and see
> What life the Gods live there, and such live thou.
>
> (V. 77-81)

The parallel with Comus is self-evident, especially in the predominance of
the "airy" or sublunar rather than celestial regions, but it goes even
further. That Satan's promis of an ascent is not an harmonious one but a
mere imitation of the "Starry Choir" is clearly demonstrated when Eve, recounting her dream to Adam, tells him,

> . . . Forthwith up to the Clouds
> With him I flew, and underneath beheld
> The Earth outstretch immense, a prospect wide
> And various: wond'ring at my flight and change
> To this high exaltation; suddenly
> My Guide was gone, and I, methought, sunk down
> And fell asleep; but O how glad I wak'd
> To find this but a dream!
>   (V. 86-93)

This is no ascent of an harmoniously inspired soul to the spheres. In her temptation to prideful ambition, Eve dreams of rising, but only to the clouds where the earth appears, not as a tiny spot, but as a broad expanse worthy to be ruled. The dream is shattered when the tempter disappears; the dreamer falls, like Alexander, the illusion broken. By contrast, when the spell of Comus is broken, the Attendant Spirit proclaims,

> Mortals that would follow me,
> Love virtue, she alone is free,
> She can teach ye how to climb
> Higher than the Sphery chime.
>   (1018-1021)

Kester Svendsen has pointed to the "choiring of _Paradise Lost_, where angelic motion and song are united to those of the spheres," as a culmination of the allusions in the nativity ode and "Arcades."[14] He cites the passage from _Paradise Lost_, V. 618-627, which has been quoted above, and makes this comment:

> "The image contains several implications central to the
> poem; the music is divine, mortal ears are too feeble
> to hear it; the music is also movement and there is an
> order to the sound like the ordered movement of the
> spheres which produce it; order is heaven's first law.
> Milton's universe is static only in its outlines; as
> many have remarked, there is movement everywhere, in
> the smallest detail of Paradise as in the great wheel
> of the universe and the inexpressive nuptial song."[15]

This orderliness is evident also in Milton's numerical organization. It will
be recalled that in the Platonic model, the harmony is that of seven spheres.
For Milton, as for Virgil, Dante, and Boethius, by including the Sphere of
the Fixed Stars and the Crystalline Sphere (as in Paradise Lost, III,
481-482), the system becomes "ninefold." However, the Sphere of the Fixed
Stars has a reverse motion, and the Crystalline Sphere is stationary.
Achilles' shield was sevenfold, but the gates of Hell are ninefold in
Miltonic terms, just as there are nine orders of angels or Heavenly intelligences according to Aristotle. Virgil's lower world was considered from the
fourth century on to consist of nine circles containing nine classes of
souls.[16] Dante, including the Primum Mobile as a sphere, had nine spheres
in the Heavens; nine circles to Hell--six in Upper Hell and three in Lower
Hell; and on the island of Purgatory nine levels with the Garden of Eden at
the top.[17] Thus Dante's Earthly Paradise is in the same position in sequence
as Milton's Crystalline Sphere.

In Paradise Lost, the discordant powers enthroned about Chaos also
number nine (in addition to Chaos before whom they sit as courtiers) in
balance with the nine harmonic spheres:

> . . . when straight behold the Throne
> Of Chaos, and his dark Pavilion spread
> Wide on the wasteful Deep; with him Enthron'd
> Sat Sable-vested Night, eldest of things,
> The Consort of his Reign; and by them stood
> Orcus and Ades, and the dreaded name
> Of Demogordon; Rumor next and Chance,
> And Tumult and Confusion all imbroil'd,
> And Discord with a thousand various mouths.
>   (II. 959-967)

As Satan first sees "this pendant world" hanging on its golden
chain, this geocentric home of man is "in bigness as a Star / Of smallest
Magnitude close by the Moon" (II. 1051-1053). But far above, God has presented His Son who will rescue that world; and the heavenly scene is made
more glorious still as it and the earthly Paradise unite where flowers of

Eden and of Heaven are one,

> And where the river of Bliss through midst of Heav'n
> Rolls o'er Elysian Flow'rs her Amber stream;
> With these that never fade the Spirits elect
> Bind their resplendent locks inwreath'd with beams,
> Now in loose Garland thick thrown off, the bright
> Pavement that like a Sea of Jasper shone
> Impurpl'd with Celestial Roses smil'd.
> Then Crown'd again thir gold'n Harps they took,
> Harps ever tun'd, that glittering by thir side
> Like Quivers hung, and with Preamble sweet
> Of charming symphony they introduce
> Thir sacred Song, and waken raptures high;
> No voice exempt, no voice but well could join
> Melodious part, such concord is in Heav'n.

(III. 358-371)

As we have noticed earlier, in discussing the nativity ode, Milton's references to the music of the spheres and to angelic choruses are often nearly inseparable. We have here a unity, not only of the music of the spheres and that of the angels, but also of the harmony of music and of color. Milton's allegory is not literal but employs the image of harmony organically so that it does not merely imitate a Pythagorean concept but develops the poet's conceived pattern of vertical and horizontal harmony in and among all facets of the universe. Harmony is not, for Milton, a merely static symbol. As Jon S. Lawry points out in his study, The Shadow of Heaven, Milton "does not hold only to the original harmony, the musica speculativa of Apollo, but considers also the achieved harmony, the musica humana attributed to Orpheus."[18] Milton's speculation does not stop with the Harmony of the Spheres alone; he uses it as a springboard to the concord of all beings and forces of creation. Milton sees harmony in colors as in sound; for he exhibits in all of his poetry a keen appreciation for the degrees of light and color in a unified rainbow, the equivalent for the harmony of variations of tone in one perfect diapason. Paradise Lost was first published in 1667. Contemporary with it were Isaac Newton's experiments with the reflecting

telescope, Robert Hooke's _Micrographia_ (1665), and Grimaldi's work with diffraction. The nature of the rainbow had intrigued imaginations since the
beginning of thought, but not until now had it been established that the
colors of the spectrum are derived from white light by diffraction. As a
new intellectual discovery would be inclined to do, this one aroused in
Milton's thinking the analogy between the scale of sound and the spectrum of
light.

The passage quoted above from _Paradise Lost_ is reminiscent as well
of the tale of Phaeton. When Phoebus has exhausted all of his warnings to
Phaeton, and the youth has insisted upon driving the chariot of the sun, the
father at last leads the way to the place where the chariot waits to be
driven out. Bulfinch tells us, "While the daring youth gazed in admiration,
the early Dawn threw open the purple doors of the east, and showed the pathway strewn with roses."[19] Bulfinch is of course dependent upon Ovid's
account that

> _Dumque ea magnanimus Phaeton miratur opusque_
> _perspicit, ecce vigil rutilo patefecit ab ortu_
> _purpureas Aurora fores et plena rosarum_
> _atria: diffugiunt stellae, quarum agmina cogit_
> _Lucifer et caeli statione novissimus exit._ (115)

The phrase _plena rosarum atria_ occurs in a number of sources, among them the
works of Cicero and Horace, in the sense of "halls filled with roses," a
closer translation than Miller's rendering, "her courts flowing with rosy
light" in the Loeb edition.[21] The bright pavement of Heaven, described by
Milton as "impurpl'd with Cèlestial Roses," owes much of its synesthetic
imagery, then, to Ovid's account.[22]

In striking contrast to all of this, however, we see that Satan has
traversed the darkness of Chaos and has come to the lowest step of the stairs
to Heaven. These stairs, by which Jacob looked upward to Heaven, are equated
with the cosmic pillar of which the Milky Way is another variant, and with
many a celestial journey by which men in dreams or visions, or their souls,
have seen the small and distant Earth and felt humbled and impressed with the

with the greater significance of the things of God.[23] Satan, however, stands
here with his back to Heaven (III. 540-543) and, like Alexander, dreams only
of conquest. Ambitious pride has led him to challenge the realm of God; and
he looks upon Earth and sees, not as Scipio saw it, so small that he was
scornful of the Roman Empire that seemed but a dot upon its surface, nor as
the ghost of Troilus perceived

> This litel spot of erthe, that with the se
> Embraced is, and fully gan despise
> This wrecched world, and held al vanite,[24]

but Satan "looks down with wonder at the sudden view / Of all this World at
once" (Paradise Lost, III. 542-543). We can fairly see him, like Alexander,
rubbing his hands together in greedy anticipation of this created universe,
a new world to conquer. He is seized with envy at the sight of the world
beneath him. For Satan, like Alexander, there is delusion of grandeur. As,
in his flight, he reaches the sun, he sees that to which his ambition-deluded
eyes ascribe great value:

> If metal, part seem'd Gold, part Silver clear;
> If stone, Carbuncle most or Chrysolite,
> Ruby or Topaz. . . .
>   (595-597)

He imagines even that he sees that stone

> Imagin'd rather oft than elsewhere seen,
> That stone, or like to that which here below
> Philosophers in vain so long have sought,
>   (598-601)

the stone sought also by Alexander on his ill-destined journey to the
heavens. Svendsen writes of this passage, "Into that brightness Satan also
deluded, brings a darkened and perverted will; all this clarity and absence
of shadow sharpen only his physical eye. The sin of the alchemists is emu-
lation of the sun; they try to short-cut the natural processes through which
God works; like Satan, they are self-deceived, and like Satan's, theirs is

finally a sin of pride."[25]

In this inversion of the celestial journey theme, Uriel is also reversed in his role as guide. Instead of being an Africanus who teaches, he is the one who is himself deceived. The earth he shows to Satan is not a spot that engenders humility, but rather "that Globe whose hither side / With light from hence, though but reflected, shine" (III. 722-723). It is "the seat of man." The spot to which he points is not small and diminished in relation to the greatness of the universe but "Paradise, / Adam's abode, those lofty shades his Bow'r" (733-734). No barely visible dot is this where even Adam's bower may be discerned. They take their leave, and Satan speeds "with hop'd success" toward "the coast of Earth beneath."

Do we have here evidence of the effect of the telescope upon man's thinking? To a very great extent it appears so, although there is precedent in the Alexander romances for Satan's view of a magnified earth rather than a diminished one. As early as the late sixteenth century, men had experimented with the "perspective glass" and had been intrigued by the way it enlarged distant landscapes so that even a particular house could be discerned. The influence of Thomas Digges was particularly evident in this respect.[26] The telescope of course played a major part in Milton's thinking. He was, as is well known, very much interested in it and visited Galileo. Some new awareness of magnitude was grasping virtually all men in the seventeenth century. The discoveries of new stars in 1572 and 1608, Galileo's Siderius Nuncius in 1610, and a stream of other new discoveries, some of which have been discussed already, could not help but enlarge man's vision. The topography of the moon also was becoming a matter of greater interest with conjectures about the possibility of life there. The seventeenth century, in the infancy of modern astronomy, was as space-conscious as we are today, and probably more astounded and amazed by it than most of us. Marjorie Nicolson has called Paradise Lost "the first modern cosmic poem, in which a drama is played against a background of interstellar space."[27] She sees a change of viewpoint, in fact, not only from earlier writers to Milton, but between

Milton's earlier poems written before he visited Galileo and this one. She
says, "the stars that shine upon his youthful poetry are still the stars of
Aristotle, undisturbed by the inruption of Tycho's or Kepler's _novae_."[28]
But in _Paradise Lost_, there is a whole new sense of perspective. As
Professor Nicolson has commented, "no preceding poet has been able to take us
in imagination to such heights, such vantage points from which, like Satan or
like God, we behold in one glance Heaven, Earth, Hell, and Space surrounding
all."[29] We might emend this to say that not before Milton have we been
shown these things on so large a scale. Hitherto, they have been seen with
the naked eye unaided by the glass of the Tuscan artist.

Soon after Satan has sped to the coast of Earth, we hear Adam and
Eve coming out of their bower to prepare for the new day; and they, too, in
this prelapsarian day, we know have heard the music of the spheres. They
enjoin the morning star and the sun to praise and acknowledge God, and
continue:

> Moon, that now meet'st the orient Sun, now fli'st
> With the fixed Stars, fixt in their Orb that flies,
> And yee five other wand'ring Fires that move
> In mystic Dance not without Song, resound
> His praise, who out of Darkness call'd up Light.
> (V. 175-179)

All music, for Milton the musician as well as poet, is for the praise of God--
the music of nature no less than that of the spheres:

> His praise ye Winds, that from four Quarters blow,
> Breathe soft or loud; . . .
> . . .
> Fountains and yee, that warble, as ye flow,
> Melodious murmers, warbling tune his praise.
> Join voices all ye living souls; . . .
> (V. 192-197)

But God, knowing the temptation about to come to Adam, sends Raphael to discourse with Adam and to increase his awareness.

Of Raphael's discourse much has been said and can be said. Not all

of it is integral to the topic here, but certain portions are closely related.
Kepler's theories of the harmonic progressions produced by the concentric
orbits of the planets may be detected in these lines, referred to earlier in
another context, where the "wheels" are described as

> Eccentric, intervolv'd, yet regular
> Then most, when most irregular they seem:
> And in their motions harmony Divine
> So smooths her charming tones, that God's own ear
> Listens delighted.
>
> (V. 623-627)

It is in the prologue to Book VII, the topic of so much debate as
to the identity of Milton's Urania, that we see Milton's guide on what has
been a celestial journey of epic proportions. What Africanus was to Scipio
and Virgil to Dante, the mysterious Urania has been to Milton:

> . . . Up led by thee
> Into the Heav'n of Heav'ns I have presum'd,
> An Earthly Guest, and drawn Empyreal Air,
> Thy temp'ring; with like safety guided down
> Return me to my Native Element:
> Lest from this flying Steed unrein'd, (as once
> Bellerophon, though from a lower Clime)
> Dismounted, on th' Aleian Field I fall
> Erroneous there to wander and forlorn.[30]
>
> (VII. 12-20)

We have mentioned Alexander's ambitious ascent and compared it with that of
Satan at the mysterious stairs. In this passage, Milton reminds us of a
similar abortive attempt to climb the heavens and join the immortals. Bellerophon, who, like Hamlet, carried a letter bearing secret instructions for his
execution, was favored by the gods by being given the winged horse Pegasus
and victory over his enemies. However, the favor shown him led to prideful-
ness. He attempted to ride Pegasus to the heavens, but Jupiter sent a gadfly
to sting the winged steed. Pegasus threw Bellerophon, who then fell to the
Aleian plains. As a result of his fall he was made lame and blind and
wandered alone in the wilderness until he died.[31]

Adam, however, in the book thus introduced, asks his great question, of how the Creation came to be, and seeks ascent to Knowledge--not out of pride, "but the more / To magnify his works, the more we know" (VII. 96-97). Raphael agrees, and we hear from his telling the melodious opening of Heaven's gates as the Creator goes out to create the "Earth self balanc't on her Centre hung" (VII. 242). Cicero tells us that "our ears have gained great delectation from the discovery and regulation of the nature and variety of sounds, and we have lifted the eyes of science to the stars, not those only which are fixed to certain spots, but those also which--not in fact, but in name--are _planet_ (_errant_). Whereof whoever was the first to observe the revolutions and movements showed that his soul was like unto Him who had fashioned them in Heaven."[32] That Milton must have had this passage in mind seems fairly probable from his mention of planets as "wand'ring Fires" (_Paradise Lost_, V. 177). Hence, there was no shame in inquiry that came from a desire to know God's works in order to praise Him the more--an important distinction to be made in the seventeenth century when in Milton's own time astronomers were under fire for heresy.

At the completion of the Creation, Raphael reminds Adam, the Creator rode again the pathway of the cosmic pillar to return to Heaven:

> . . . Up he rode
> Follow'd with acclamation and the sound
> Symphonious of ten thousand Harps that tun'd
> Angelic harmonies: the Earth, the Air
> Resounded, (thou remember'st, for thou heard'st)
> The Heav'ns and all the Constellations rung,
> The Planets in thir station list'ning stood,
> While the bright Pomp ascended jubilant.
> (VII. 557-564)

Here again, for Milton, angels and stars sing together in a perfect harmony between these different parts of the heavenly creation.

The all-penetrating interest in science that has been seen to occupy the thinking of Milton's day shows again when Raphael pauses in his account of Creation to comment to Adam upon the stars "numerous, and every Star

perhaps a World / Of destin'd habitation" (VII. 621-622). Even so, Adam is
not guilty here of the sin of pride. His geocentric world still consists of
Heaven and

> . . . this Earth a spot, a grain,
> An Atom, with the Firmament compar'd
> And all her number'd Stars, that seem to roll
> Spaces incomprehensible (for such
> Thir distance argues and thir swift return
> Diurnal) merely to officiate light
> Round this opacous Earth, this punctual spot,
> One day and night.
> (VIII. 17-24)

To him, Earth is still the pin prick, the tiny spot of either place or time,
the punctum from which our words "puncture" and punctual" both derive--still
the little threshing floor it appeared to Dante and to Chaucer's Troilus.
And "his countenance seem'd / Ent'ring on studious thoughts abstruse"
(39-40).

Adam is puzzled. But Raphael perceives that he is troubled in
part because he confuses size and value. Adam must not think that because
Earth is so small it is of little worth:

> . . . consider first, that Great
> Or Bright infers not Excellence: the Earth
> Though, in comparison of Heav'n, so small,
> Nor glistering, may of solid good contain
> More plenty than the Sun that barren shines,
> Whose virtue on itself works no effect,
> But in the fruitful Earth.
> (VIII. 90-96)

Still, he goes on to assure Adam,

> Yet not to Earth are those bright Luminaries
> Officious, but to thee Earth's habitant.
> And for the Heav'n's wide Circuit, let it speak
> The Maker's high magnificence, who built
> So spacious, and his Line stretcht out so far;
> That Man may know he dwells not in his own;

> An Edifice too large for him to fill,
> Lodg'd in a small partition, and the rest
> Ordain'd for uses to his Lord best known.
>   (98-106)

Here is Milton's point, then: that the smallness of Earth in relation to the size of the whole universe does not diminish its importance; and, by inference from that, man's smallness in Creation does not reduce his value. Neither, however, does his centricity vaunt him, for God's universe stretches so far that man cannot hope to dwell in more than a small portion or room, as it were, of it. The rest is for the uses of God, which only He knows. We are reminded here of Origen, who interpreted much of the Bible as allegory, and his view of the spheres as the mansions of Heaven of which Jesus spoke when He said, "In my Father's House are many mansions."[33]

There is room yet for conjecture by man. The new theories of astronomy have not been discarded, nor the old cast away:

> . . . What if the Sun
> Be Centre to the World, and other Stars
> By his attractive virtue and thir own
> Incited, dance about him various rounds?
>   (122-125)

Milton's reference here to the "attractive virtue" of the sun is again a strong indicator of the influence of Kepler. In the fourth book of the Epitome of Copernican Astronomy (1618-1621),[34] Kepler is concerned with the nature of the spheres, the ratios of the planets to each other, the position of the sun in the center where it can vivify and illuminate the planets. The spheres, he says, are not solid: comets cut through from one to another, light coming through them is not refracted, and their eccentric orbits do not interfere with each other. The planets therefore must be kept in their orbits by a force since they do not ride the spheres like chariots and do not have wings to fly like birds. This force, he concludes, is exerted by the sun in the central position and is magnetic in nature, so that "repulsion and attraction take place according to the lines of virtue going out from the centre of the sun; and since these lines revolve along with the sun, it is necessary for the planet too which is repelled and attracted to follow these lines in proportion to their strength in relation to the resistance of the planetary body."[35] Each planet also has its own magnetic force or "attractive virtue" so that it responds to that of the sun.

What if the sun be in the center, asks Milton's Raphael, and what if the earth move? This must be so, says Kepler, even aside from the scientific reasons arising from the sun's functions as illuminator, vivifier, and governor; for the harmony of the universe, which he calls "the soul and life of all astronomy," can be complete "only if the Earth in its own place and rank among the planets strikes its own note through a variation of a semitone: otherwise there would be no manifesting of its semitone, and that again is the soul of the song. As a matter of fact, if the semitone of the Earth is gone, there is destroyed from among the celestial movements the manifesting of the genera of song, i.e., the major and the minor modes, the most pleasant, most subtle, and most wonderful thing in this whole discussion."[36] In like manner, Milton emphasizes throughout Paradise Lost, if man be not enlivened and illuminated and moved by God, Who is the center of his life, then too is the harmony of the Creation incomplete by the absence of man's major and minor modes. In the terms of Boethius, harmony exists in three forms: mundana, humana, and instrumentis.[37] All three must work together. As for Milton the harmony of the angels and that of the spheres is unified, so is the harmony of the world and that of man, so that in the end all are one.

The twenty or so lines following those we have examined in Raphael's conversation with Milton's Adam are replete with "what if," "if Land be there" (on the moon), and "perhaps." The day of conjecture has arrived in greater measure than ever before. Man's curiosity is reaching out through Galileo's telescope. To the seventeenth century this is not a little frightening, and cautious minds, with Raphael, warn the children of Adam,

> Solicit not thy thoughts with matters hid,
> Leave them to God above, him serve and fe. *r*;
> Of other Creatures, as him pleases best,
> Wherever plac't, let him dispose; joy thou
> In what he gives to thee, this Paradise
> And thy fair _Eve_: Heav'n is for thee too high
> To know what passes there; be lowly wise:
> Think only what concerns thee and thy being;
> Dream not of other Worlds.
>
> (VIII. 167-175)

But men did dream of other worlds in the seventeenth century, and they still do. Adam, child of simplicity, exclaims, "How fully has thou satisfied me, pure / Intelligence of Heav'n, Angel serene," (180-181); but his children have never ceased in "Mind or Fancy . . . to rove Uncheckt" (188-189).

NOTES

[1] _John Milton_: Complete Poems and Major Prose, ed., Merritt Y. Hughes (New York: Odyssey Press, 1957). All quotations from the works of John Milton are from this edition and are cited in parentheses in the text.

[2] Archibald Macleish, "Mankind's Image May Be Remade," New York Times News Service (Tucson: Arizona Daily Star, December 25, 1968), p. A-2.

[3] Marjorie Nicolson, "The Telescope and Imagination," Modern Philology, 32 (1935), 233-60; p. 233.

[4] Ibid., p. 234.

[5] Ibid., p. 235.

[6] Arthur O. Lovejoy, The Great Chain of Being (Cambridge, Massachusetts: Harvard University Press, 1942), pp. 101-102.

[7] A very small difference of pitch.

[8]Johannes Kepler, The Harmonies of the World, V, trans. Charles
Glenn Wallis, in Great Books of the Western World, Vol. 16 (Chicago:
Encyclopedia Britannica, Inc., 1952), p. 1031. I have divided the chart
into three sections in order to present each section with the discussion of
it.

[9]Ibid, p. 1039.

[10]Ibid, pp. 1017-1018.

[11]Marjorie Nicolson, John Milton: A Reader's Guide to his Poetry
(New York: Farrar, Straus, and Giroux, 1963), p. 33.

[12]Platonica Theologica, VII. 36. See footnote, Hughes edition of
Milton (fn. 1 above), p. 81.

[13]"There is a high way, easily seen when the sky is clear. 'Tis
called the Milky Way, famed for its shining whiteness. By this way the gods
fare to the halls and royal dwelling of the mighty Thunderer. On either side
the palaces of the gods of higher rank are thronged with guests through
folding-doors flung wide. The lesser gods dwell apart from these. Fronting
on this way, the illustrious and strong heavenly gods have placed their
homes. This is the place which, if I may make bold to say it, I would not
fear to call the Palatia of high heaven."

Ovid, Metamorphoses, I. 168-176, ed. Frank Justus Miller (Cambridge,
Massachusetts: Harvard University Press [Loeb Library], 1916), pp. 14-15.
All references to Ovid are from this edition unless otherwise noted.

[14]Kester Svendsen, Milton and Science (Cambridge, Massachusetts:
Harvard University Press, 1956), pp. 60-61.

[15]Ibid., p. 61.

[16]La Divina Commedia di Dante Alighieri, ed., C. H. Grandgent
(Boston: Heath, 1933), fn., p. 5.

[17]Ibid., pp. vi-viii.

[18]Jon S. Lawry, The Shadow of Heaven (Ithaca: Cornell Univ. Press, 1968), p. 25.

[19]Thomas Bulfinch, The Age of Fable of Beauties of Mythology, ed., Reverend J. Loughran Scott (Philadelphia: David McKay, 1898), p. 54.

[20]Metamorphoses II, 111-115, p. 68.

[21]Ibid., p. 69.

[22]Henry T. Riley, in The Metamorphoses of Ovid (London: George Bell and Sons [Bohn's Classical Library], 1881), renders the passage thus: "And while the aspiring Phaëton is admiring these things [i.e., the workmanship of the chariot of the sun], and is examining the workmanship, behold! the watchful Aurora opened her purple doors in the ruddy east, and her halls filled with roses. The stars disappear, the troops whereof Lucifer gathers, and moves the last from his station in the heavens" (p. 49). Bulfinch paraphrases the account and tells us that "the early Dawn threw open the purple doors of the east, and showed the pathway strewn with roses" (p. 54).

[23]See Chapter I, p. 3-4.

[24]Geoffrey Chaucer, "Troilus and Criseyde," V. 1821, The Works of Geoffrey Chaucer, ed., F. N. Robinson, 2nd Ed. (Boston: Houghton Mifflin, 1957), p. 479.

[25]Milton and Science, pp. 126-127.

[26]Francis R. Johnson, Astronomical Thought in Renaissance England (Baltimore: Johns Hopkins Press, 1937), pp. 176-177.

[27]Marjorie Nicolson, "Milton and the Telescope," ELH, 2:1 (April, 1935), 1-32; p. 3.

[28]Ibid., p. 4.

[29]Ibid., p. 15.

[30]Among others, William B. Hunter's article, "Milton's Urania" in SEF (4:1 Winter, 1964 , 35-42) is important here. Hunter discusses the problem of the identification of the muse, especially in regard to her as the Uranian Aphrodite or Heavenly Beauty of Plato's Symposium. She is Mind, he says, the first Emanation of the One, as inspiration for poets as well as the Muse of Astronomy.

[31]Bulfinch, p. 157.

[32]Cicero, Tusculan Disputations 1:25, The Basic Works of Cicero, ed., Moses Hadas (New York: Modern Library, 1951), pp. 92-93.

[33]See pages 24-25 for discussion of Origen. Much of Milton's theology is influenced by his study of the writings of Origen, the "grand-father" of Arianism. From Origen, also, comes the concept basic to the idea of an eternal and immanent Trinity within which the Son's existence is "increate" (see Paradise Lost, III. 1-12, the "Invocation to Light" and V. 594 ff. in which the Son is described as the essence of that light imbosomed within the orbs), coexistent with the Father from eternity and unto eternity. Origen speaks of the "logos" as the educator of the souls in the spheres. Milton, in The Christian Doctrine (p. 933), says that "the Son existed in the beginning, under the name of the logos or word, and was the first of the whole creation, by whom afterwards all other things were made both in heaven and earth."

[34]Johannes Kepler, Epitome of Copernican Astronomy, IV. in Great Books of the Western World, Volume 16, pp. 845-960.

[35]Ibid., p. 935.

[36]Ibid., p. 913.

[37]Boetii (Boethius), De Institutione Arithmetica, Libri Duo; De Institutione Musica, Libri Quinque, ed., Godofredus Friedlein, 1867 (Lipsiae: Minerva G.M.B.H., 1966). De Institutione Musica, I, ii, pp. 187-189.

CHAPTER VI

THE EMPYRAEUM OF PURE HARMONY

> . . . [T]hus, bravely thus
> (Fraught with a fury so harmonious)
> The Lutes light <u>Genius</u> now does proudly rise,
> Heav'd on the surges of swolne Rapsodyes.
> Whose flourish (Meteor-like) doth curle the aire
> With flash of high-borne fancyes: here and there
> Dancing in lofty measures, and anon
> Creeps on the soft touch of a tender tone:
> Whose trembling murmurs melting in wild aires
> Runs to and fro, complaining his sweet cares
> Because thos pretious mysteryes that dwell,
> In musick's ravish't soule hee dare not tell,
> But whisper to the world: thus doe they vary
> Each string his Note, as if they meant to carry
> Their Masters blest soule (snatcht out at his Eares)
> By a strong Exstasy) through all the sphaeres
> Of Musicks heaven; and seat it there on high
> In th' <u>Empyraeum</u> of pure Harmony.
> At length (after so long, so loud a strife
> Of all the strings, still breathing the best life
> Of blest variety attending on
> His fingers fairest revolution
> In many a sweet rise, many as sweet a fall)
> A full-mouth <u>Diapason</u> swallowes all.
> (Richard Crashaw, "Musicks Duell,"
> lines 133-156)[1]

During most of the seventeenth century, references to the celestial journey and the Harmony of the Spheres fall into two main categories, though there are, of course, many exceptions. The celestial journey tends to become almost entirely a journey of the soul toward God as part of a formal exercise of contemplation. It is in the state of "exstasy" that the soul detaches itself from the limitations of the body, ascends into the spheres to the empyraeum for a union with God, and, purified thereby, returns to the body and imparts purification to the life of the contemplating worshipper. The Harmony of the Spheres, with the increasing acceptance of the idea of the heliocentric universe and with the development of increasingly sophisticated and efficient telescopes, became a metaphor of the process of that purification gained by the soul in ecstacy. It came to express the longstanding concepts of harmony and unity within the universe as a symbol of that harmony and unity between God and man, between men, and within a man. For some poets, of course, both the celestial journey and the music of the spheres became merely a conceit without any deeper significance than an expression for the love of a lover for his lady.

With the advent of the new astronomy, the Book of Nature became more and more a means of learning God's nature. Sir Thomas Browne tells us in _Religio Medici_,

> Thus there are two books from whence I collect my divinity: besides that written one of God, another of His servant nature-- that universal and public manuscript that lies expansed unto the eyes of all. Those that never saw Him in the one have discovered Him in the other. This was the Scripture and theology of the heathens: the natural motion of the sun made them more admire Him than its supernatural station did the children of Israel; the ordinary effects of nature wrought more admiration in them than in the other (did) all His miracles. Surely the heathens knew better how to join and read these mystical letters than we Christians, who cast a more careless eye on these common hieroglyphics and disdain to suck divinity from the flowers of nature. Nor do I so forget God as to adore the name of Nature, which I define not with the schools (as) the principle of motion and rest, but that straight and regular line, that settled and constant course the wisdom of God hath ordained (for) the actions of His creatures according to their several kinds. To make a revolution every day is the nature of the sun because (of) that necessary course which God hath ordained it, from which it cannot swerve but by a faculty from that Voice which first did give it motion.[2]

For Sir Thomas Browne, it is evident that the new astronomy with the sun as

as the center of the universe has not become the rule, though in 1634-1637
when he was composing it, that system could not have been unknown to him.
Again, the old remains the metaphor in all likelihood, the means of expression even when the new is "known"--much as we today, in fact, still
speak of sunrise and sunset. For Sir Thomas Browne, the importance of the
idea itself lies in its significance for representing to men the truth of
God. For him, the world--the universe--is truly Theocentric, regardless of
its astronomy:

> That God made all things for man is in some sense true, yet
> not so far as to subordinate the creation of those purer
> creatures [i.e., the angels, of which he has spoken in the
> portion just preceding this] unto ours, though as ministering
> spirits they do, and are willing to fulfill the will of God
> in these lower and sublunary affairs of man. God made
> all things for Himself, and it is impossible He should make
> them for any other end than His own glory. It is all He can
> receive, and all that is without Himself. For honor being
> an eternal adjunct and in the honorer rather than in the
> person honored, it was necessary to make a creature from
> whom He might receive this homage, and that is in the other
> world angels, in this, man. Which, when we neglect, we forget
> the very end of our creation and may justly provoke God not
> only to repent that He hath made the world but that He hath
> sworn He would not destroy it.[3]

It makes little difference for such writers as Milton, Donne, Crashaw, Sir
Thomas Browne whether the planets revolve about the earth or about the sun.
Whichever may be so, in the final analysis they revolve about God.

For John Donne, the ecstacy of contemplation and the human ecstasy
of love could be joined in the expression of human love, an imitation of
Love as a divine principle. His poem "The Ecstasy" need not be given here
in illustration; but the thought seems apparent that for Donne there is that
which is divine in that which is human in action, and both may be expressed
in the same terms. In "Good Friday, 1613, Riding Westward," the concept of
devotion as a guiding principle of man's soul just as the "intelligences"
who guided the spheres can be considered their souls:

> Let man's soul be a sphere, and then, in this,
> The intelligence that moves, devotion is,
> And as the other spheres, by being grown
> Subject to foreign motions, lose their own,
> And being by others hurried every day,
> Scarce in a year their natural form obey,
> Pleasure or business, so our souls admit
> For their first mover, and are whirled by it.

It is Christ's crucifixion that "made His own lieutenant Nature shrink,
It made His footstool crack. / Could I behold those hands which span the
poles, / And tune all spheres at once, pierced with those holes?"[4]

In the "Hymn to God my God, in my Sickness," Donne views death as
unity with the music of the spheres:

> Since I am coming to the holy room
> Where, with Thy choir of saints forevermore,
> I shall be made Thy Music, as I come
> I tune the instrument here at the door,
> And what I must do then, think now before.

As for Milton, for Donne the music of the spheres and the music of the angels
are one. Furthermore, the death of the body becomes the birth of the soul
and its coming, not just into the presence of Christ but into compelte unity
with the harmony of Heaven so as to become an integral part of it. In
preparation for death, then, he tunes the instrument--prepares his soul for
its new life, its entrance into that unity by contemplating upon what his
entrance into the heavenly harmony will be like. This is not fear of dying
but preparation for it by close analysis of each of its steps. As the sun
sets in the West as part of its natural course, so, says Donne,

> I joy, that in these straits, I see my West;
> For, though their current yield return to none,
> What shall my West hurt me? As West and East
> In all flat maps (and I am one) are one,
> So death doth touch the resurrection.

If "west" is death, then "east" is birth; and as the death of the body is

the birth of the soul, and west and east are unified at the edges of a flat
map, the poet then is joyous in his recognition that death and birth are one.

> So, in His purple wrapped, receive me, Lord,
> By these His thorns give me His other crown;
> And as to others' souls I preached Thy word,
> Be this my text, my sermon to mine own,
> Therefore that He may raise, the Lord throws down.

That the ideas within this concept of the Harmony of the Spheres
and the many interpretations of that "harmony" became a means of expressing
more earthly unities is apparent in Lovelace's "Gratiana Dauncing and
Singing" from Lucasta (1649). Here, the harmony is expressed as gracefulness,
the unity as rhythmic motion:

> I
> SEE! with what constant Motion
> Even, and glorious, as the Sunne,
>   Gratiana steeres that Noble Frame,
> Soft as her breast, sweet as her voyce
> That gave each winding Law and poyze,
>   And swifter then the wings of Fame.

> II
> She beat the happy Pavement
> By such a Starre made Firmament,
>   Which now no more the Roofe envies;
> But swells up high with Atlas ev'n,
> Bearing the brighter, nobler Heav'n,
>   And in her, all the Dieties.

> III
> Each step trod out a Lovers thought
> And the Ambitious hopes he brought,
>   Chain'd to her brave feet with such arts,
> Such sweet command, and gentle awe,
> As when she ceas'd, we sighing saw
>   The floore lay pav'd with broken hearts.

> IV
> So did she move; so did she sing
> Like the Harmonious spheres that bring
>   Unto their Rounds their musick's ayd;

> Which she performed such a way
> As all th'inamour'd world will say
>   The Graces daunced, and Apollo play'd.[5]

As John Hollander comments, it is the dancing of Gratiana that "affords room for invention" of the conventions of the harmony here. "But even the heavenly spheres, like the strings plucked by Crashaw's lutenist, are described as dancing to their own song; they are dancers primarily, and their singing is subordinated to their graceful movement."[6]

John Dryden offers one of the best examples in the late seventeenth century of the purposes for which the concept of the Harmony of the Spheres was becoming useful. As a metaphor for the divine plan, the unity and true harmony of creation, it became the means of expressing the fundamental design of the universe:

> From harmony, from heavenly harmony
> This universal frame began;
> When nature underneath a heap
> Of jarring atoms lay,
> And could not heave her head,
> The tuneful Voice was heard from high,
> 'Arise, ye more than dead.'
>
> Then cold, and hot, and moist, and dry,
> In order to their stations leap,
> And Music's pow'r obey.
> From harmony, from heav'nly harmony
> This universal frame began:
> From harmony to harmony
> Thro' all the compass of the notes it ran,
> The diapason closing full in Man.
>
>   II
> What passion cannot Music raise and quell!
> When Jubal struck the corded shell,
> His list'ning brethren stood around,
> And, wond'ring, on their faces fell
> To worship that celestial sound.
> Less than a god they thought there could not dwell
> Within the hollow of that shell
> That spoke so sweetly and so well.
> What passion cannot Music raise and quell!

III

The Trumpet's loud clangor
Excites us to arms,
With shrill notes of anger,
And mortal alarms.
The Double double double beat
Of the thund'ring Drum
Cries 'Hark! the foes come;
Charge, charge, 'tis too late to retreat.'

IV

The soft complaining Flute
In dying notes discovers
The woes of hopeless lovers,
Whose dirge is whisper'd by the warbling Lute.

V

Sharp Violins proclaim
Their jealous pangs, and desperation,
Fury, frantic indignation,
Depths of pains, and heights of passion,
For the fair, disdainful dame.

VI

But O! what art can teach,
What human voice can reach,
The sacred Organ's praise?
Notes inspiring holy love,
Notes that wing their heav'nly ways
To mend the choirs above.

VII

Orpheus could lead the savage race;
And trees unrooted left their place,
Sequacious of the lyre;
But bright Cecilia rais'd the wonder high'r:
When to her Organ vocal breath was giv'n,
And angel heard, and straight appear'd,
Mistaking earth for heav'n.

Grand Chorus

As from the pow'r of sacred lays
The spheres began to move,
And sung the great Creator's praise
To all the blest above;
So, when the last and dreadful hour

This crumbling pageant shall devour,
The Trumpet shall be heard on high,
The dead shall live, the living die,
And Music shall untune the sky.[7]

   This 1687 ode that celebrates the day in honor of St. Cecilia,
patron saint of music and especially of organs, organists, and church music
in general, is one of the most frequently quoted poems on the subject of the
music of the spheres. The universe, the poet begins, is built upon the
principle of harmony--heavenly harmony, the archetypal harmony of which that
on earth is an imitation. Before the universe there was only chaos, "when
nature underneath a heap / Of jarring atoms lay." Nature was unable to lift
her head until summoned by the heavenly harmony. Thus Nature--Natura--is
subservient to the Harmony of the Spheres, to the universal music of Creation,
and dependent upon it. Without that harmony, nature is more than dead because she is uncreated, has not even begun to exist.

   The first things in the creation, says Dryden, were the elements--
cold, hot, moist, and dry--and they as well obeyed the summons of the
heavenly harmony, are dependent upon that music for their beginning. From
the ordering of the elements out of Chaos, harmony as the creating power of
God went from one part of the universe to another, and the diapason--the full
octave, the full range--closed full on Man. In a full diapason on an organ,
the full capacity of the organ is employed. It is the stop expressing rich-
ness above all others. In man, then, this creative power of Harmony expressed all of the harmonies that had been expressed in part in the other
facets of creation.

   Jubal, in Genesis 4:21, is called the father of those who handle
the harp and the organ, the inventor of wind and stringed instruments.
Dryden tells us here of the origin of these instruments in the simple sea-
shell held to the ear--a "celestial sound" coming, not through the agency
of man but of nature as the agent, in turn, of God. It seems, in fact, to
be the abode of a god.

He turns then to the capabilities of the various types of instrumental music to "raise and quell" the passions--to stimulate and to calm: the clangor of the trumpet, the dirge of the flute and the lute, the sharpness of violins. But of them all, the organ, as the voice that combines all, is the one closest to the heavenly harmony. As the heavenly harmony combines all others, musica mundana, human, and instrumentis alike, so the organ combines on earth the voices of percussion and wind and string. Even the human voice cannot surpass the capabilities of the "sacred Organ's praise" even so far as to "mend the choirs above," to surpass the angels. Orpheus, whose music could so entrance that he could win back Eurydice from death by his music, whom trees were said to follow when he played his lyre, is surpassed by St. Cecilia's organ; for an angel who heard her mistook earth for heaven and suddenly appeared.

The culmination of the poem is in many respects a peak of intensity, a climax for the idea of the Harmony of the Spheres itself. In this Grand Chorus the poet proclaims that, just as the power of this harmony was the instigating power for the first motions of the spheres, so shall it order the last of "this crumbling pageant." The motions of the spheres, inspired by the heavenly harmony, have from the beginning sung the praise of God. It is they, says Dryden, who sing to the angels themselves. At the last, he says, when the trumpet calls, the order shall change. It will not be destroyed utterly--this is not, I believe, a return to Chaos in the darkest sense of that word, but a reordering. The dead shall live and the living die. Like Donne, perhaps, Dryden tells us that West and East shall meet. Death and Birth are unified in the Resurrection. When that comes, there is no further need for music as we know it; for all is true harmony in the perfection that must follow the final day of judgment and resurrection. Music shall untune the sky--not return it to chaotic disorder but return it to the perfect state before the universal harmony itself set the elements in their stations.

NOTES

[1]The Poems, English Latin and Greek, of Richard Crashaw, ed., L. C. Martin (Oxford: Clarendon Press, 1957), pp. 149-155.

[2]Sir Thomas Browne, Religio Medici, ed., Frank L. Huntley (New York: Appleton, Century, Crofts, 1966), pp. 19-20. Note: Words in parentheses above are added by the editor in this edition.

[3]Ibid., p. 44.

[4]Poems by John Donne are from the edition of John Donne's Poetry by A. L. Clements (New York: W. W. Norton, 1966).

[5]Richard Lovelace, Poems, ed., L. H. Wilkinson (Oxford: Oxford University Press, 1930), p. 25.

[6]John Hollander, The Untuning of the Sky: Ideas of Music in English Poetry, 1500-1700 (Princeton, New Jersey: Princeton Univ. Press, 1961), pp. 343-344.

[7]"A Song for St. Cecilia's Day, 1687," John Dryden, in The Poetical Works of John Dryden (Boston: Houghton Mifflin Company Cambridge Edition , 1909, pp. 252-253.

EPILOGUE

In the late eighteenth century certain elements of Platonism and
Neoplatonism reemerged in the intellectual atmosphere—ideas of the World
Soul, the Celestial Journey, the Music of the Spheres, Platonic Love, and
others. These emerged, however, as fragments, discrete notions, symbols,
not as components of coherent philosophical and theological systems. The
world view of which they were once essential elements had dissolved with the
acceptance of Copernican astronomy and Newtonian science. They served
rather, in arts and letters at least, as metaphors, similes, dream mechanisms,
or as convential allegorical topoi.[1]

Yet the essential distinction between the pre-Romantic and the
Romantic use of such elements is not, it must be emphasized, their largely
metaphorical, non-literal, allegorical role in the work of the Romantics.
Few if any of the great poets of the older world-view gave to its ruling
concepts a merely or chiefly "literal" signification. From Hesiod through
Ovid, Dante, and Spenser to Milton, such "concepts," such "myths" were
rather symbols, metaphors, allegories of religious and philosophical truths.
Literal acceptance of the actuality of the music of the spheres and of the
celestial journey—however ingenious the arguments for their actuality—
belongs rather to the mental and cultural matrix we today call "shamanism."
Admittedly, even the greater minds were not altogether liberated from this
matrix—one in which Orthodox Christian belief has been involved from the
beginning of our era until today. Yet certainly, as among the ancients, the
movement of thought and art has been toward symbolic and allegorical render-
ings of the "gods" and credos of religion and philosophy.

As we have said, the "great tradition" of Platonic and Neoplatonic
ideology, whether in its Christian or other metamorphoses, that had been

139

continued and expressed in the earlier eras by poets as free from naivete,
if less informed on the facts of cosmography, as those of the eighteenth
and nineteenth centuries, now again made its influence felt in English
poetry. Most clearly is this influence apparent in the work of Shelley, one
of a temperament of a mind in tune with the idea-images of celestial music and
and ascent.

Upon the elder generation of the English Romantics, this influence
is incidental, even to be termed superficial. Such passages as these that
follow from the less temperamental Wordsworth and the more eclectic Coleridge
can be matched only with difficulty , if at all, from the corpus of their
works.

In the _Prelude_, higher minds who deal with the whole compass of
the universe

>   . . . for themselves create
> A like existence: and whene'er it dawns
> Created for them, catch it or are caught
> By its inevitable mastery,
> Like angels stopped upon the wing by sound
> Of harmony from Heaven's remotest spheres.
>   (xiv, 94-99)

In the memorable "Mutability" sonnet of his _Ecclesiastical_ sequence,
Wordsworth curiously associates Henry VIII's dissolution of the monasteries
with the music of the spheres:

> From low to high doth dissolution climb,
> And sink from high to low, along a scale
> Of awful notes, whose concord shall not fail;
> A musical but melancholy chime,
> Which they can hear who meddle not with crime,
> Nor avarice, nor over-anxious care.
> Truth fails not; but her outward forms that bear
> The longest date do melt like frosty rime,
> That in the morning whitened hill and plain
> Of yesterday, which royally did wear
> His crown of weeds, but could not even sustain
> Some casual shout that broke the silent air,
> Or the unimaginable touch of Time (III, xxxiv)

In Colerdige, as later in Shelley, the "Platonic" and "Christian"
concepts and images of celestial harmony and ascent are blended with others
of various origins and significance, some modern, contemporary, others as
"traditional" as those the course of which in English poetry we have been
following. Notable among these are the idea-images of the Aeolian Harp and
the Rainbow. The poet finds

> . . . one Life within us and abroad,
> Which meets all motion and becomes its soul,
> A light in sound, a sound-like power in light,
> Rhythm in all thought, and joyance everywhere--
> Methinks, it should have been impossible
> Not to love all things in a world so fill'd;
> Where the breeze warbles, and the mute still air
> Is Music slumbering on her instrument.
> (The Aeolian Harp, 26-33)

In his Ode to the Departing Year, Colerdidge hails the

> Spirit who sweepest the wild Harp of Time!
> It is most hard, with an untroubled ear
> Thy dark inwoven harmonies to hear!
> (1-3)

It is in the work of Shelley that something of the vitality, the
potency, if not the more or less logical coherence, of the traditional complex of celestial music and ascent returns into English poetry. The loci
classici in his major poems are familiar, but still deserve attention if not
analysis. It would be a mistake, however, to look upon Shelley's incomplete,
infrequent, and brief "intimations" of the harmony of the spheres and the
ascent through them to the Empyrean as ever crystallizing into any sort of
coherent philosophical or poetic system. Shelley was "enraptured," one
might say, with an often blended light and music and motion;[2] but in his
verses these are chiefly, if not exclusively, the light and music and motion
of the World of Nature. Expressions of celestial harmonies of light and
sound and motion occur only intermittently until the final stages of his

brief career. Explicit echoes of "celestial" music apart from that of the
sphere of the Moon are rare; explicit recountings of journeys to the Empyrean
through the nine spheres of the heavens are not to be found in the corpus of
his verse.

Queen Mab and The Revolt of Islam foreshadow in occasional verses
the movement of Shelley's thought and imagination through a labyrinth,
almost a chaos, of notions modern and traditional, toward the somewhat
clearer and more "Platonic" but still distinctly "modern" and "Shelleyan"
vision of Nature, Man, and Eternity expressed in Prometheus Unbound and
Adonais.

In Queen Mab, as Mab and the Spirit of Ianthe look down, they see

> . . . high on an isolated pinnacle;
> The flood of ages combating below,
> The depth of the unbounded universe
> Above, and all around
> Nature's unchanging harmony.
> (II. 253-257)

Obvious here is the influence of the Newtonian view of the cosmos. The
harmony is that of Nature, not that of a transcendent realm. Somewhat
closer to the pre-Newtonian world view are these verses in which Ianthe's
soul is shown standing before heavenly bodies:

> Countless and unending orbs
> In mazy motion intermingled,
> Yet still fulfilled immutably
> External Nature's law.
> Above, below, around,
> The circling systems formed
> A wilderness of harmony;
> Each with undeviating aim,
> In eloquent silence, through the depths of space
> Pursued its wondrous way.
> (II. 73-82)

Yet "the circling systems" form, most curiously, a "wilderness of harmony,"
and utter no music but that of "eloquent silence"! Possible allusions to

the Music of the Spheres may be found in certain verses of <u>To a Skylark</u> and
in this couplet in Shelley's last poem, <u>The Triumph of Life</u>:

> The world can hear not the sweet notes that move
> The sphere whose light is melody to lovers.
> (478-479)

The idea-image of the Music of the Spheres, if not that of the
Celestial Journey, moves toward a somewhat clearer expression in such
familiar verses as these in <u>Prometheus Unbound</u>:

> Meanwhile thy spirit lifts its pinions
> In music's most serene dominions;
> Catching the winds that fan that happy heaven.
> And we sail on, away, afar,
> Without a course, without a star,
> But, by the instinct of sweet music driven;
> Till through Elysian garden islets
> By thee, most beautiful of pilots,
> The boat of my desire is guided:
> Realms where the air we breathe is love,
> Which in the winds and on the waves doth move,
> Harmonizing this earth with what we feel above.
> (II., v., 85-96)

Yet the "spirits" sail on "without a course, without a star," driven by the
"instinct of sweet music"--notions hardly Christian, Platonic, or Neoplatonic! Perhaps one source is to be found elsewhere. Carl Grabo observed--
following Hargraves Jennings, a nineteenth century student of Rosicrucian
notions--in Rosicrucian thought a parallel to Shelley's apotheosis of music,
and quoted Jennings in support of such a view:

> The whole world is taken as a musical instrument; that
> is, a chromatic, sensible instrument. The common axis
> or pole of the world celestial is intersected--where
> this superior diapason or heavenly concord or chord
> is divided--by the spiritual sun, or center of sentience.
> Every man has a little spark (sun) in his own bosom.
> Time is only protracted consciousness, because there
> is no world out of the mind conceiving it. Earthly
> music is the faintest tradition of the angelic state;

> it remains in the mind of man as the dream of, and
> the sorrow for, the lost paradise. Music is yet
> master of the man's emotions, and therefore of the
> man.[3]

Notwithstanding the ambivalence of such passages and the paucity, almost the absence, of explicit allusions to the Music of the Spheres and the Celestial Journey in Shelley's poems, there are still at least two major and recurrent and increasingly clear and poetic expressions of the preoccupation of his imagination with these great themes and symbols. First of these, as Grabo following Jennings may be telling us, are the poet's evocations of the music of the universe—music indeed chiefly of the realm of Nature, the music of the winds and waters, of birds, of all growing and animate creatures—evocations that achieve their climactic expression in the triumphal and antiphonal strophes of the orbs of the Earth and Moon in the closing strophes of Prometheus Unbound. A major source for the mind and imagination of Shelley, it can hardly be doubted, in such passages must have been the concept and the image of the Music of the Spheres.

A search or sounding for echoes, rare new births, sproutings as it were in uncongenial modern soil, of the concepts and images of Celestial Music and Ascent in the post-Romantic era, is an undertaking to be offered to others. Yet few and thin as the sprouts that may appear, what might be called, somewhat paradoxically, their subterranean vitality and potency still remain. Of such vitality and potency Shelley's verse, if only in a minor degree, is an expression for his era. Even today, one can believe that the roots in the life and culture of the less tutored, of the "shamanistic" rituals and beliefs so fully analyzed by Mircea Eliade continue strong and enduring. Most adherents to the great world religions still accept either with literal belief, or with more or less sophisticated rationales, concepts and images close to those of the Music of the Spheres and the Celestial Journey.

More apparent and more significant for the student of literature are the "temporalizing," the "secularizing," which our themes and images have undergone since the Romantic Era.[5] Strangely enough, they have experienced a sort of scientific and technological realization, at times perhaps a kind of demonic parody, both in so-called "science fiction" and in the familiar "heavenly utopias," the roots of which extend into antiquity. And what note is to be taken of the actual voyages of our time, manned or unmanned, into outer space? Or of the reputed recording by radar of the "music" of the planets and even far distant stars and galaxies?

Less "secularized," perhaps, although certainly "temporalized," are the sometimes parallel, sometimes widely divergent, poetic accounts of the "Ascent of Man" through the ages to be found in the work of Tennyson and Whitman and certain of their successors. Again, it is for others to continue the already advanced assessment of the degrees of Darwinian, traditional Christian although hardly Platonic, and Oriental influences in their rhapsodic statements of such "ascent" and to determine the degree of relationship to the great tradition the course of which has been traced in the foregoing chapters.

A. G.

NOTES

[1]The primary sources consulted by Dr. Hammil during her consideration of her themes in "Post-Dryden" English literature appear, at least in part, in the following pages. Among major secondary sources are these: James A. Notopoulos, The Platonism of Shelley (Durham, N. C., 1949); ed., L. J. Zillman, Shelley's Promotheus Unbound: A Variorum Edition (Seattle, Washington, 1959); Earl R. Wasserman, Shelley: A Critical Reading (Baltimore, Maryland, 1971); Carl Grabo, Prometheus Unbound: An Interpretation (Chapel Hill, N. C., 1935).

[2]Such "blending," usually termed "synaesthesia," a phenomenon both psychological and poetic, occurs frequently in Shelley and also in Keats. It has, however, only a peripheral relationship to the central themes of the Music of the Spheres and the Celestial Journey. More closely related are the theme and imagery of the "dance" of the heavenly spheres, which have not been specifically considered by Dr. Hammil. A full consideration of their place in this complex of concepts and images is an obvious desideratum.

[3]Carl Grabo, Prometheus Unbound: An Interpretation (Chapel Hill, N. C., 1935), p. 90.

[4]Earl Wasserman has described the spirit of the Earth as an equivalent of one of the Platonic Intelligences that guide the spheres—an all-embracing

> love that guides and is the joyous animating spirit
> of the earth: *'L'amour che move il sole e l'altre
> stella.* Shelley's "Prometheus Unbound", (Baltimore:
> Johns Hopkins Press, 1965), p. 74.

Shelley, Wasserman argues, has given Asia the identity of Venus. Eros, the son of Venus, is presented by Earth as her "torch-bearer." In the final act Eros or Love is fused with or replaces Earth, and may also be identified with a heavensent guide to the celestial spheres.

In these same triumphal passages one senses also an outflowing of the concept-image of the "spheres," which in earlier pre-Romantic poetry joined in celestial harmony, concordia discors. The emphasis indeed is upon the roles of two of the "spheres," the orbs of Earth and Moon—the other seven having, apparently, receded in Shelley's imagination into the all-encompassing realms of Nature. Yet both the music and the images of light link the poet's achievement here surely with the great tradition descending from antiquity through Dante, Spenser, Milton, and Dryden.

No brief summation can do justice, of course, to the complexity and ambivalence of Shelley's imagery in these and other passages in his poems.

One may note, in _passus_ only, how in its astronomical aspect it exhibits a paradoxical fusion of the cosmographies of Ptolemy and Copernicus. Further one must enter the caveat that the _Prometheus Unbound_ like its predecessors and successors in Shelley's poetry is above all a Poem of Revolution, both terrestrial and beyond the Earth throughout the Universe. Only so, the poet seems to be declaring, can the "harmony of the spheres" be finally consummated. The achievement of a more complete account and analysis of these vital and potent aspects of Shelley's imaginative world must remain, however, as a challenge to oncoming students of his verse and thought.

Beyond the _Prometheus Unbound_ the final and culminating expression of Shelley's "Romantic" and highly personal "Platonism" is to be found, as all students are aware, in certain of the closing stanzas of his _Adonais_. Yet even here the "celestial music" is not a song of joy, of the harmony of the spheres, but a dirge of Urania, "most musical of mourners," voicing a terrestrial loss and sorrow. The ascent to heavenly realms is expressed not in the sequence of Dante's _Paradiso_, but in terms of a related complex of ideas and images—that so brilliantly analyzed by A. O. Lovejoy in his _Great Chain of Being_. Shelley's utterances is clearest, most "Platonic" in Stanzas 42 through 44 and in these earlier proud verses—

> . . . . the spirit shall flow
> Back to the burning fountain whence it came,
> A portion of the Eternal, which must glow
> Through time and change, unquenchably the same. . .
> (xxxviii, 339-341)

[5]Cf. A. O. Lovejoy's consideration of the temporalizing of the concepts of plenitude and continuity, those of the great chain of being in the closing chapters of his classical work so entitled.

BIBLIOGRAPHY

I.   CLASSICAL AND GENERAL

Aristotle.   Meteorologica.   Trans. H. D. P. Lee.   Cambridge, Massachusetts:
     Harvard University Press (Loeb Library), 1952.

Aristotle.   On the Heavens. Trans., W. K. C. Guthrie.   Cambridge,
     Massachusetts: Harvard University Press (Loeb Library), 1939, 1960.

Barnes, Hazel E.   "Unity in the Thought of Empedocles."   Classical
     Journal 63:1 (October, 1967), 18-23.

Brewer, Wilmon.   Ovid's Metamorphoses in European Culture.   Boston:
     Cornhill, 1933.

Bulfinch, Thomas.   The Age of Fable or Beauties of Mythology.   Revised ed.
     by Reverend J. Loughran Scott.   Philadelphia: David McKay, 1898.

Chappell, William.   The History of Music (Art and Science).   Volume I,
     From Earliest Records to the Fall of the Roman Empire.   London:
     Chappell and Company, n.d.   1874 preface .

Cicero, Marcus Tullius.   Cicero's Three Books of Offices or Moral Duties.
     Ed., Cyrus R. Edmonds.   New York: Harper, 1899.

Cicero, Marcus Tullius.   The Basic Works of Cicero.   Ed., Moses Hadas.
     New York: Modern Library, 1951.

Cicero, Marcus Tullius.   De Re Publica, De Legibus.   Trans., Clinton
     Walker Keyes.   Cambridge, Massachusetts: Harvard University
     Press (Loeb Library), 1928.

Cicero, Marcus Tullius. *Tusculan Disputations I and Scipio's Dream*. Ed.,
  Frank Ernest Rockwood. Norman: University of Oklahoma Press,
  1903, 1966.

Coleman-Norton, P. R. "Cicero and the Music of the Spheres," *Classical
  Journal* 45:5 (February, 1950), 237-241.

Cornford, Francis MacDonald. *Plato's Cosmology: The Timaeus of Plato
  Translated with a Running Commentary*. London: Routledge and
  Kegan Paul, 1937.

Crashaw, Richard. *The Poems, English Latin and Greek of Richard Crashaw*,
  Ed., L. C. Martin. 2nd ed. Oxford: Clarendon Press, 1957.

Curtius, Ernst Robert. *European Literature and the Latin Middle Ages*.
  Trans., W. R. Trask. New York: Harper, 1953; Harper Torchbook
  Edition, 1963.

De La Mare, Walter. *Behold This Dreamer*. London: Faber and Faber, 1939.

Dreyer, J. L. E. *A History of Astronomy from Thales to Kepler*. 2nd ed.
  New York: Dover, 1953.

Durant, Will. *Caesar and Christ*. New York: Simon and Schuster, 1944.

Eliade, Mircea. *The Sacred and the Profane: The Nature of Religion*. Trans.,
  Willard R. Trask. New York: Harper and Row, Torchbook Edition,
  1961.

Eliade, Mircea. *Myths, Dreams, and Mysteries*. Trans., Philip Mairet.
  New York: Harper and Brothers, 1960.

Farrington, Benjamin. *Greek Science: Its Meaning for Us*. Baltimore:
  Penguin, 1953.

Friedländer, Paul. *Plato*. 3 volumes. Trans., Hans Meyerhoff. Princeton,
  New Jersey: Princeton University Press (Bollingen Series LIX),
  1958-1969.

Grochio, Johannes de. Concerning Music. Colorado Springs: Colorado College Music Press, 1967.

Guthrie, W. K. C. A History of Greek Philosophy. 4 volumes. Cambridge: Cambridge University Press, 1962.

Harrison, Jane. Prolegomena to the Study of Greek Religion. New York: World Publishing Company (Meridian), 1959.

Heath, Sir Thomas. Aristarchus of Samos, the Ancient Copernicus. Oxford: Clarendon Press, 1913.

Highbarger, Ernest Leslie. The Gates of Dreams: An Archaeological Examination of Vergil, Aeneid VI, 893-899. Baltimore: Johns Hopkins Press, 1940.

Highet, Gilbert. The Classical Tradition: Greek and Roman Influences on Western Literature. Oxford: Oxford University Press, 1949.

Johnson, Francis Rarick. Astronomical Thought in Renaissance England: A Study of English Scientific Writings from 1500 to 1645. Baltimore: Johns Hopkins Press, 1937.

Jolles, Andre. Einfache Formen, Legende, Sage, Mythe, Rätsel, Spuch, Kasus, Memorabile, Märchen, Witz. Tübingen, 1958.

Jones, Richard Foster. Ancients and Moderns: A Study of the Rise of the Scientific Movement in Seventeenth Century England. Berkeley: University of California Press, second edition, 1961.

Kahn, Charles H. Anaximander and the Origins of Greek Cosmology. New York: Columbia University Press, 1960.

Kepler, Johann. Kepler's Conversation with Galileo's Sidereal Messenger. Trans., Rosen. (Sources of Science Number 5). New York: Johnson Reprint Company, 1965.

Kepler, Johann. Mysterium Cosmographicum. Ed. 2. München: C. H. Beck, 1963.

King, H. C.   Exploration of the Universe.   New York: New American Library
(Signet), 1964.

Kocher, Paul H.   Science and Religion in Elizabethan England.   San Marino,
California: Huntington Library, 1953.

Koestler, Arthur.   The Sleep Walkers: A History of Man's Changing Vision of
the Universe.   New York: Macmillan, 1959.

Kuhn, Thomas S.   The Copernican Revolution: Planetary Astronomy in the
Development of Western Thought.   New York: Random House (Vintage),
1957.

Láng, Paul Henry.   Music in Western Civilization.   New York: Columbia
University Press, 1941.

Lucan.   The Civil War [Pharsalia].   Trans., J. D. Duff.   New York:
G. P. Putnam's Sons (Loeb Library), 1928.

Macrobii, Ambrosii Theodosii.   Commentarii in Somnium Scipionis.   Ed.,
Iacobus Willis.   Leipzig: Aedibus B. G. Teubneri, 1963.

Macrobio, Teodosio.   Somnium Scipionis Commentarios.   Turin, Italy:
Unione Tipografico, 1967.

Macrobius: Commentary on the Dream of Scipio.   Trans. and ed., William
Harris Stahl.   New York: Columbia University Press, 1952.

McKinney, Howard D. and W. R. Anderson.   Music in History: The Evolution
of an Art.   New York: American Book Company, 1940.

Mei, Girolamo.   Letters on Ancient and Modern Music to V. Galilei and
G. Bardi.   New York: American Institute of Musicology, 1960.

Moutsopoulos, Evanghélos.   La Musique dans L'oeuvre de Platon.   Paris:
Presses Universitaires de France, 1959.

Nicolson, Marjorie.   "The Telescope and Imagination."   Modern Philology 32
(1935), 233-260.

Nock, A. D. _Sallustius: Concerning the Gods and the Universe_. Cambridge: Cambridge University Press, 1926.

Ovid. _Metamorphoses_. Trans., Justus Miller. Cambridge, Massachusetts: Harvard University Press (Loeb Library), 1916.

Ovid. _The Metamorphoses of Ovid_. Trans. and ed., Henry T. Riley. London: George Bell and Sons (Bohn's Classical Library), 1881.

Petersson, Torsten. _Cicero: A Biography_. Berkeley: University of California Press, 1920.

Plato. _The Dialogues of Plato_. Trans., B. Jowett, 4th edition. Oxford: Clarendon Press, 1953.

Plato with an English Translation. Volume VII: _Timaeus_, _Critias_, _Cleitophon_, _Menexenus_, _Epistles_. Trans., R. G. Bury. New York: G. P. Putnam's Sons (Loeb Library), 1929.

Pliny. _Natural History_. Trans., H. Rackham. Cambridge, Massachusetts: Harvard University Press (Loeb Library), 1949.

Plotinus. _The Enneads_. Trans., Stephen MacKenna. Second Edition. London: Faber and Faber, Oxford University Press, 1956.

Plutarch. _Moralia_. Fifteen volumes. Trans., Benedict Einarson and Phillip H. DeLacy. Cambridge, Massachusetts: Harvard University Press (Loeb Library), 1967.

Porter, Jermain G. _The Stars in Song and Legend_. Boston: Ginn and Company, 1901.

Ptolemy, _The Almagest_: _On the Revolutions of the Heavenly Spheres_, by Nicolaus Copernicus; _Epitome of Copernican Astronomy_: IV and V. _The Harmonies of the World_: V, by Johannes Kepler. Chicago: Encyclopaedia Britannica, Inc. (Great Books of the Western World), 1938–1939.

Ratcliff, Arthur James John. A History of Dreams; a Brief Account of the
    Evolution of Dream Theories, with a Chapter on the Dream in
    Literature. Boston: Small, Maynard and Company, 1923.

Reichel-Dolmatoff, Gerardo. Amazonian Cosmos: The Sexual and Religious
    Symbolism of the Tukano Indians. Chicago: University of Chicago
    Press, 1971.

Rose, H. J. A Handbook of Latin Literature. New York: E. P. Dutton, 1960.

Rougier, Louis Auguste Paul. La Religion Astrale des Pythagoricians.
    Paris: Presses Universitares de France, 1959.

Ross, Sir W. D. Aristotle's Physics. Oxford: Oxford University Press, 1936.

Salinas, Francisco. De Musica. Documenta Musicologica XIII. (Facsimile).
    Kessel und Basel: Barenreiler-Verlag, 1958.

Spitzer, Leo. Classical and Christian Ideas of World Harmony. Ed.,
    A. G. Hatcher. Baltimore: Johns Hopkins Press, 1963.

Starnes, De Witt Talmadge and Ernest William Talbert. Classical Myth and
    Legend in Renaissance Dictionaries. Chapel Hill: University of
    North Carolina Press, 1955.

Thorndike, Lynn. The 'Sphere' of Sacrobosco and its Commentators.
    Chicago: University of Chicago Press, 1949.

Zuckerkandl, Victor. Sound and Symbol: Music and the External World.
    Trans., Willard R. Trask. New York: Pantheon Books
    (Bollingen Series, XLIV), 1956.

II. MEDIAEVAL PERIOD

Alexander, The Prose Life of: from the Thornton MS. Ed., J. S. Westlake.
    London: Kegan Paul (Early English Text Society), 1913 (for 1911).

Baker, Donald C. "The Parliament of Fowls," in _Companion to Chaucer Studies_. Ed., Beryl Rowland. Oxford, Oxford University Press, 1968.

Barrett, Helen M. _Boethius: Some Aspects of his Times and Work_. New York: Russell and Russell, 1965.

Bennett, J. A. W. _Chaucer's Book of Fame_. Oxford: Clarendon Press, 1968.

Bennett, J. A. W. _The Parliament of Foules: An Interpretation_. Oxford: Clarendon Press, 1957.

Bloomfield, Morton. "Distance and Predestination in _Troilus and Criseyde_." PMLA 72 (1957), 25.

Boethii, Anicii Manlil Torquati Severini. _De Institutione Arithmetica, Libri Duo_; _De Institutione Musica, Libri Quinque_. Ed., Godofredus Friedlein. Leipzig: Minerva G.M.R.H., 1966.

Boethius. _The Theological Tractates_. Trans., H. F. Stewart and F. K. Rand; _The Consolation of Philosophy_. Trans., H. F. Stewart. New York: G. P. Putnam's Sons (Loeb Library), 1926.

Boethius. _The Consolation of Philosophy_. Trans., Richard Green. New York: Bobbs-Merrill (Library of Liberal Arts), 1962.

Bolgar, R. R. _The Classical Heritage and its Beneficiaries_. Cambridge: Cambridge University Press, 1954.

Bonaventura, Saint. _The Mind's Road to God_. Trans. George Boas. New York: Bobbs-Merrill (Library of Liberal Arts), 1953.

Cary, George. _The Medieval Alexander_. Cambridge: Cambridge University Press, 1956

Chaucer, Geoffrey, _The Works of Geoffrey Chaucer_. Ed., F. N. Robinson. Boston: Harcourt Brace, 1957.

Chaucer, Geoffrey. _The Complete Works of Geoffrey Chaucer_. Ed., W. W. Skeat. Oxford: Clarendon Press, 1894-1897.

Clark, John W. "Dante and the Epilogue of _Troilus_." JEGP 50 (1951), 1-10.

Courcelle, Pierre. _La Consolation de Philosophie dans la Tradition_
  Litteraire: Antecedents et Posterite de Boece. Paris: Etudes
  Augustiniennes, 1967.

Curry, Walter Clyde. _Chaucer and the Mediaeval Sciences_, second edition.
  New York: Barnes and Noble, 1960.

Dante. _The Vision; or Hell, Purgatory, and Paradise_. Trans., H. F. Cary.
  New York: Worthington, 1844.

Dante. _La Divina Commedia_. Ed., C. H. Grandgent, revised edition.
  Boston: Heath, 1933.

Dante. _The Comedy of Dante Alighieri the Florentine_. Three volumes.
  Trans., Dorothy L. Sayers. Baltimore: Penguin Books, 1955.

Dante. _The Divine Comedy_. Volume III, _Paradiso_. Trans., John D. Sinclair.
  New York: Oxford (Galaxy), 1961.

Denis, M. J. _De La Philosophie D'Origène_. Paris: L'Imprimerie Nationale,
  1884.

David, Alfred. "_The Hero of the Troilus_." _Speculum_ 37 (1962), 570.

Dronke, Peter. "The Conclusion of _Troilus and Criseyde_." MAE 33 (1964),
  48ff.

Dunbar, H. Flanders. _Symbolism in Medieval Thought_. New Haven, Connecticut:
  Yale University Press, 1929).

Durant, Will. _The Age of Faith_. New York: Simon and Schuster, 1950.

Fergusson, Francis. _Dante's Dream of the Mind: a Modern Reading of the_
  Purgatorio. Princeton, New Jersey: Princeton University Press,
  1953.

Gögler, Rolf. _Zur Theologie des Biblischen Wortes bel Origenes_.
  Dusseldorf: Patmos-Verlag, 1963.

Hieronymus de Moravia, OP. _Tractatus de Musica_. Ed., Dr. Simon M. Cserba. Regensburg: Friedrich Pustet, 1935.

Huppé, Bernard F. and D. W. Robertson, Jr. _Fruyt and Chaf_: _Studies in Chaucer's Allegories_. Princeton, New Jersey: Princeton University Press, 1963.

Koonce, B. G. _Chaucer and the Tradition of Fame_: _Symbolism in the House of Fame_. Princeton, New Jersey: Princeton University Press, 1966.

Lewis, C. S. _The Allegory of Love_. Oxford: Oxford University Press, 1936, 1968.

Lewis, C. S. _The Discarded Image_. Cambridge: Cambridge University Press, 1964, 1967.

Lovejoy, Arthur O. _The Great Chain of Being_: _A Study of the History of an Idea_. Cambridge, Massachusetts: Harvard University Press, 1936

Lydgate's Fall of Princes. Ed., Henry Bergen. Four volumes. Oxford: Oxford University Press (Early English Text Society), 1924.

Malone, Kemp. _Chapters on Chaucer_. Baltimore: Johns Hopkins Press, 1951.

McCall, John P. "Troilus and Criseyde," in _Companion to Chaucer Studies_. E., Beryl Rowland. Oxford: Oxford University Press, 1968, pp. 370-384.

McDonald, Charles O. "An Interpretation of Chaucer's _Parlement of Foules_." In Chaucer: _Modern Essays in Criticism_. Ed., Edward Wagenknecht. New York: Oxford University Press, 1959.

Medieval Philosophy: _From St. Augustine to Nicholas of Cusa_. Ed., John F. Wippel and Allan B. Wolter, O.F.M. New York: The Free Press, 1969

Meech, Sanford B. _Design in Chaucer's Troilus_. Syracuse, New York: Syracuse University Press, 1959.

Origen. On First Principles: Being Koetschau's Text of the De Principils. Trans., G. W. Butterworth. New York: Harper and Row (Torchbook), 1966.

Patch, Howard Rollin. The Goddess Fortuna in Mediaeval Literature. Cambridge, Cambridge, Massachusetts: Harvard University Press, 1927.

Patch, Howard Rollin. The Tradition of Boethius: A Study of His Importance in Medieval Culture. New York: Oxford University Press, 1935.

Patch, Howard Rollin. "Troilus on Predestination," JEGP 17 (1918), 399-423. In Chaucer: Modern Essays in Criticism. Ed., Edward Wagenknecht. New York: Oxford University Press, 1959.

Patch, Howard Rollin. "Troilus on Determinism." Speculum 6 (1929), 225-243. In Chaucer Criticism, Vol. 2, Ed., R. J. Schoeck and J. Taylor. Notre Dame, Indiana: Notre Dame Paperbacks, 1961.

Reiss, Edmund. "Troilus and the Failure of Understanding," MLQ 29:2 (June, 1968), 131-144.

Robertson, D. W. Jr. "Chaucerian Tragedy." In Chaucer Criticism, Vol. 2, Ed., R. J. Schoeck and J. Taylor. Notre Dame, Indiana: Notre Dame Paperbacks, 1961.

Tatlock, J. S. P. "The Epilog of Chaucer's Troilus." Modern Philology. 18 (1921), 625-659.

Wells, John Edwin. A Manual of the Writings in Middle English 1050-1400. New Haven: Yale University Press, 1916.

White, T. H. The Bestiary: A Book of Beasts, Being a Translation from a Latin Bestiary of the Twelfth Century. New York: G. P. Putnam's Sons, 1960.

III. ENGLISH RENAISSANCE

Agar, Herbert. Milton and Plato. Princeton, New Jersey: Princeton
University Press, 1928; Oxford University Press, 1931.

Allen, Don Cameron. The Harmonious Vision: Studies in Milton's Poetry.
Enlarged edition. Baltimore: Johns Hopkins Press, 1970.

Baldwin, Edward C. "Milton and Plato's Timaeus." PMLA 35 (1920), 210-217.

Browne, Sir Thomas. Religio Medici. Ed., Frank L. Huntley. New York:
Appleton Century Crofts, 1966.

Bush, Douglas. Classical Influences on Renaissance Literature. Cambridge,
Massachusetts: Harvard University Press, 1952.

Bush, Douglas. Mythology and the Renaissance Tradition in English Poetry.
Revised edition. New York: W. W. Norton, 1964.

Coffin, Charles Monroe. John Donne and the New Philosophy. New York:
Humanities Press, 1958.

Collins, Joseph B. Christian Mysticism in the Elizabethan Age. Baltimore:
Johns Hopkins Press, 1940.

Craig, Hardin. An Interpretation of Shakespeare. Columbia, Missouri:
Lucas Brothers, 1948.

Craig, Hardin. The Enchanted Glass: The Elizabethan Mind in Literature.
New York: Oxford University Press, 1936.

Curry, Walter Clyde. Milton's Ontology, Cosmogony, and Physics. Lexington:
University of Kentucky Press, 1957.

Curry, Walter Clyde. Shakespeare's Philosophical Patterns. Baton Rouge:
Louisiana State University Press, 1937, 1959.

Donne, John. John Donne's Poetry. Ed., A. L. Clements. New York:
W. W. Norton, 1966.

Dryden, John. The Poetical Works of John Dryden. Boston: Houghton Mifflin (Cambridge Edition), 1909.

Elizabethan Reader, the Portable. Ed., Miram Haydn. New York: Viking Press, 1946.

Elson, Louis C. Shakespeare in Music. Boston: L. C. Page Company, 1900.

Gilbert, Allen H. "Milton's Textbook of Astronomy." PMLA 38 (1923), 297-307.

Gilbert, Allen H. "Milton and Galileo." Studies in Philology 19 (1922), 152-185.

Gower, John. Confessio Amantis: The English Works of John Gower. Two volumes. Ed., G. C. Macaulay. Oxford: Oxford University Press (Early English Text Society), 1900.

Granville-Barker and G. B. Harrison. A Companion to Shakespeare Studies. New York: Doubleday, 1960.

Hanford, James Holly. A Milton Handbook. Revised edition. New York: F. S. Crofts, 1933.

Harrison, G. B. Shakespeare: The Complete Works. New York: Harcourt Brace, 1948.

Holland, Norman N. The Shakespearean Imagination. New York: Macmillan, 1964.

Hollander, John. The Untuning of the Sky: Ideas of Music in English Poetry, 1500-1700. Princeton, New Jersey: Princeton University Press, 1961.

Hughes, Merritt Y. "Lydian Airs." MLN 60 (1925), 129-137.

Hunter, William B. "Milton's Urania." SEL 4:1 (Winter, 1964), 35-42.

Johnson, Samuel, ed. The Works of the English Poets from Chaucer to Cowper; Including the Series Edited, With Prefaces, Biographical and Critical, by Dr. Samuel Johnson; and the Most Approved Translations.

The Additional Lives by Alexander Chalmers, F.S.A. Twenty-one volumes. London: Printed for J. Johnson et al. by C. Whittingham, 1810.

Kirkconnell, Watson. The Celestial Cycle: The Theme of Paradise Lost in World Literature With Translations of the Major Analogues. Toronto: University of Toronto Press, 1952.

Knight, G. Wilson. The Crown of Life. London: Methuen, 1948.

Knight, G. Wilson. The Imperial Theme: Further Interpretations of Shakespeare's Tragedies Including the Roman Plays. New York: Barnes and Noble, 1951. London: Methuen, 1949.

Knight, G. Wilson. The Wheel of Fire: Interpretations of Shakespearean Tragedy. London: Methuen, 1949.

Knobel, E. B. "Astronomy and Astrology" in Shakespeare's England, two volumes. Oxford: Oxford University Press, 1917. Volume I, 444-461.

Long, John H., ed. Music in English Renaissance Drama. Lexington: University of Kentucky Press, 1968.

Long, John H. Shakespeare's Use of Music: A Study of the Music and its Performance in the Original Production of Seven Comedies. Gainesville: University of Florida Press, 1955.

Lovelace, Richard. Poems. Ed., L. H. Wilkinson. Oxford: Oxford University Press, 1930.

MacCaffrey, Isabel Gamble. Paradise Lost as "Myth". Cambridge, Massachusetts: Harvard University Press, 1967.

Madsen, William G. From Shadowy Types to Truth: Studies in Milton's Symbolism. New Haven: Yale University Press, 1968.

McAlindon, T. "Language, Style, and Meaning in Troilus and Cressida." PMLA 84 (January, 1969), 29-43.

McColley, Grant. "The Astronomy of Paradise Lost." SP 34 (1937), 209-247.

Milton, John. Complete Poems and Major Prose. Ed., Merritt Y. Hughes. New York: Odyssey Press, 1957.

Murry, John Middleton. Shakespeare. New York: Harcourt. Brace, 1936.

Nicolson, Marjorie. John Milton: A Reader's Guide to his Poetry. New York: Farrar, Straus, and Giroux, 1963.

Nicolson, Marjorie. "Milton and the Telescope." ELH 2 (1935), 1-32.

Nicolson, Marjorie. "The Telescope and English Imagination," SP July, 1935.

Nitchie, Elizabeth. Vergil and the English Poets. New York: Columbia University Press, 1919.

Notopoulos, James A. The Platonism of Shelley. Durham, North Carolina: Duke University Press, 1949.

Orchard, Thomas N. The Astronomy of Milton's "Paradise Lost". London: Longman, Green, 1896.

Poetry of the English Renaissance, 1509-1660. J. William Hebel and Hoyt H. Hudson, Eds., New York: F. S. Crofts, 1929

Robins, Harry F. "Satan's Journey: Direction in Paradise Lost." Milton Studies in Honor of H. F. Fletcher. Urbana: University of Illinois, 1961.

Ross, Lawrence J. "Shakespeare's 'Dull Clown' and Symbolic Music." Shakespeare Quarterly 61:2 (Spring, 1966), 109-128.

Samuel, Irene. Plato and Milton. Ithaca: Cornell University Press, 1947.

Saurat, Denis. Milton: Man and Thinker. New York: Dial Press, 1925.

Seventeenth Century Prose and Poetry, second edition. Ed., Alexander M. Witherspoon and Frank J. Warnke. New York: Harcourt Brace and World, 1929, 1963.

Silver Poets of the Sixteenth Century. Ed., Gerald Bullett. New York:
      E. P. Dutton (Everyman Library), 1947.

Smith, Marion Bodwell. Dualities in Shakespeare. Toronto, Canada:
      University of Toronto Press, 1966.

Snider, Denton J. System of Shakespeare's Dramas. Two volumes. St. Louis:
      G. I. Jones and Company, 1877.

Spalding, K. J. The Philosophy of Shakespeare. Oxford: George Roland, 1953.

Spencer, Theodore. Shakespeare and the Nature of Man. New York: Macmillan,
      1942.

Spenser, Edmund. The Complete Poetical Works of Spenser. Ed., R. E. Neil
      Dodge. Boston: Houghton Mifflin (Cambridge Edition), 1908.

Spurgeon, Caroline. Shakespeare's Imagery and What it Tells Us. Cambridge:
      Cambridge University Press, 1935.

Stauffer, Donald A. Shakespeare's World of Images. New York: W. W. Norton,
      1949.

Svendsen, Kester. Milton and Science. Cambridge, Massachusetts: Harvard
      University Press, 1956.

Thomson, J. A. K. Shakespeare and the Classics. London: Allen and Unwin,
      1952.

Tillyard, E. M. W. "The Cosmic Background" in Approaches to Shakespeare.
      Ed., Norman Rabkin. New York: McGraw-Hill, 1954.

Tillyard, E. M. W. The Elizabethan World Picture. New York: Random House
      (Vintage Books), n.d.

Tillyard, E. M. W. Studies in Milton. New York: Macmillan, 1951. London:
      Chatto and Wingus, 1955.

Tuve, Rosamund. Images and Themes in Five Poems by Milton. Cambridge,
      Massachusetts: Harvard University Press, 1957.

164

Tuva, Rosamund. _Allegorical Imagery_: _Some Mediaeval Books and Their
        Posterity_. Princeton, New Jersey: Princeton University Press,
        1966.

Whiting, George Wesley. _Milton and this Pendant World_. Austin: University
        of Texas Press, 1958.

Willey, Basil. _The Seventeenth Century Background_. New York: Doubleday
        (Anchor), 1935.

IV.   ROMANTIC AND MODERN PERIODS

Abercrombie, Lascellas. _The Art of Wordsworth_. Oxford University Press,
        1952.

Abrams, M. H., editor. _English Romantic Poets_. Oxford University Press,
        1960.

Abrams, M. H. _The Mirror and the Lamp_: _Romantic Theory and the Critical
        Tradition_. New York: W. W. Norton, 1958.

Adair, Patricia M. _The Waking Dream: A Study of Coleridge's Poetry_.
        New York: Barnes and Noble, 1968.

Baker, Carlos Heard. _Shelley's Platonic Answer to a Platonic Attack on
        Poetry_. Iowa City: University of Iowa Press, 1965.

Balslev, Thora. _Keats and Wordsworth, A Comparative Study_. Copenhagen:
        Munksgaard, 1962.

Bate, Walter Jackson. _From Classic to Romantic_. New York: Harper and Row,
        1946.

Barfield, Owen, _Poetic Diction_: _A Study in Meaning_. New York: McGraw-Hill,
        1928, 1964.

Barnard, Ellsworth. _Shelley's Religion_. Minneapolis: University of
        Minnesota Press, 1936.

Beer, John Bernard. _Coleridge the Visionary_. New York: Collier Books, 1959, 1962.

Benziger, James. _Images of Eternity: Studies in the Poetry of Religious Vision from Wordsworth to T. S. Eliot_. Carbondale: Southern Illinois University Press, 1962.

Bloom, Harold. _Shelley's Mythmaking_. New Haven: Yale University Press, 1959.

Bloom, Harold. _The Visionary Company: A Reading of English Romantic Poetry_. London: Faber and Faber, 1962.

Boulger, James D. _Coleridge as Religious Thinker_. New Haven: Yale University Press, 1961.

Bowra, C. M. _The Romantic Imagination_. Cambridge: Harvard University Press, 1949.

Bush, Douglas. _Mythology and the Romantic Tradition in English Poetry_. Cambridge: Harvard University Press, 1937.

Bush, Douglas. "Keats and His Ideas," _English Romantic Poets_. M. H. M. H. Abrams, ed. Oxford University Press, 1960.

Chesser, Dr. Eustace. _Shelley and Zastrozzi: Self Revelation of a Neurotic_. London: Gregg/Archive, 1965.

Crompton, Margaret. _Shelley's Dream Women_. London: Cassell, 1967.

Edmunds, Edward William. _Shelley and His Poetry_. London: G. G. Harrap, 1911

Evert, Walter. _Aesthetic and Myth in the Poetry of Keats_. Princeton University Press, 1965.

Ferry, David. _The Limits of Mortality: An essay on Major Poems_. Middletown, Conn.: Wesleyan University Press, 1965.

Fogle, Richard Harter. _The Imagery of Keats and Shelley_. University of North Carolina Press, 1949.

Gerard, Albert S. English Romantic Poetry: Ethos, Structure and Symbol in Coleridge, Wordsworth, Shelley and Keats. Berkeley: University of California Press, 1968.

Gingerich, Solomon Francis. Essays in the Romantic Poets. New York: Macmillan, 1924.

Grabo, Carl. The Meaning of the "Witch of Atlas". Chapel Hill: University of North Carolina Press, 1935.

Grabo, Carl. A Newton Among Poets: Shelley's Use of Science in Prometheus Unbound. University of North Carolina Press, 1930.

Grabo, Carl. Prometheus Unbound: An Interpretation. University of North Carolina Press, 1935.

Hoffman, Harold Leroy. An Odyssey of the Soul, Shelley's Alastor. New York: Columbia University Press, 1933.

Hughes, A. M. D. The Nascent Mind of Shelley. Oxford University Press, 1947.

Hunt, Leigh. The Indicator, August 2, 1822. Leight Hunt's Examiner Examined as quoted from Abrams' The Mirror and the Lamp.

Huxley, Aldous, editor. The Autobiography and Memoirs of Benjamin Haydon. London, I, 1926, New York: Harcourt Brace, n.d.

Jones, F. L. "The Vision Theme in Shelley's Alastor and Related Works." SP, LXIV (1947), 1969.

Kauvar, Gerald B. The Other Poetry of Keats. Rutherford: Fairleigh Dickinson University Press, 1969.

Keppler, Carl Francis. The Problem of Symbolism in the Ancient Mariner. Tucson: University of Arizona Press, 1951.

Knight, G. Wilson. The Starlit Dome. Oxford University Press, 1941

Knight, William Angus, editor. Wordsworthiana, A Selection from Papers
   Read to the Wordsworth Society. New York: Macmillan, 1889.
   Especially the following essays: J. H. Shorthouse, "The Platonism
   of Wordsworth"; R. S. Watson, "Wordsworth's Relations to Science";
   W. A. Heard, "Wordsworth's Treatment of Sound."

Lowes, John Livingston. The Road to Xanadu. Boston: Houghton Mifflin, 1927.

Lyon, Judson Stanley. The Excursion: A Study. New Haven: Yale University
   Press, 1950.

Marsh, Florence. Wordsworth's Imagery, A Study in Poetic Vision.
   New Haven: Yale University Press, 1952.

Murray, Roger N. Wordsworth's Style: Figures and Themes in the Lyrical
   Ballads of 1800. Lincoln: University of Nebraska Press, 1967.

Notopoulos, James A. The Platonism of Shelley. Durham, North Carolina:
   Duke University Press, 1949.

O'Malley, Glenn. "Shelley's Air-Prism: The Synesthetic Scheme of Alastor".
   MP, LV (1958), 178-187.

O'Malley, Glenn. Shelley and Synesthesia. Evanston, Illinois: Northwestern
   University Press, 1964.

Palacio, J. L., editor. "Music and Musical Themes in Shelley's Poetry."
   MLR, LIX (1964), 345-359.

Perkins, David. The Quest for Performance: The Symbolism of Wordsworth,
   Shelley, and Keats. Cambridge: Harvard Press, 1959.

Piper, H. W. The Active Universe. London: Athlone, 1962.

Reiman, Donald H. Shelley's "The Triumph of Life": A Critical Study.
   Urbana: University of Illinois Press, 1965.

Rossetti, William Michael. Shelley's Prometheus Unbound Considered as a
   Poem. London: Privately printed, 1887.

Santayana, George. Interpretations of Poetry and Religion.
New York: Härper and Row, 1957.

Shawcross, John, editor. Shelley's Literary and Philosophical Criticism.
London: Henry Frowde, 1909.

Shelley, Percy B. The Complete Poetical Works of Percy Shelley. George
Edward Woodberry, editor, 4 Volumes. Boston: Houghton Mifflin, 1892.

Stawell, Florence Melian. Shelley's "Triumph of Life." Oxford: Oxford
University Press, 1914.

Wasserman, Earl R. Shelley: A Critical Reading. Baltimore: Johns Hopkins
Press, 1971.

Wasserman, Earl R. Shelley's "Prometheus Unbound." Baltimore: Johns
Hopkins Press, 1965.

Wasserman, Earl R. The Subtler Language. Baltimore: Johns Hopkins
Press, 1959.

Willey, Basil. The Eighteenth Century Background. London: Chatto & Windus,
1940. Boston: Beacon Press, 1961.

Williams, Charles. The English Poetic Mind. New York: Russell and Russell,
1963.

Winstanley, Lilian. Platonism in Shelley. Oxford: Oxford University Press,
1913.

Woodman, Ross Grieg. The Apocalyptic Vision in the Poetry of Shelley.
Toronto: University of Toronto Press, 1964.

Zillman, L. J., editor. Shelley's "Prometheus Unbound": A Variorum Edition.
Seattle, Washington: University of Washington Press.

Zwerdling, Alexander, "The Mythographers and the Romantic Revival of Greek
Myth." PMLA, LXXIX (1964), 447-456.

INDEX